BOAT

TALES

*True Stories of Fishing,
Hunting, and Outdoors Adventures*

Gordon England

BOOKS BY GORDON ENGLAND

Searching for One Particular Harbour
Escape to the Bahamas

MORE STORIES AND PHOTOS AT
www.islandtales.biz

First printing 2010
Copyright © 2010 Gordon England
Second printing January 2012
Third printing July 2013

ISBN-13: 978-1451515084

ii

Boat Tales

For my wife, Annie, a lover of life.
Without her, most of these stories would not be.
She is my soul mate and kindred partner. She is fearless
on the ocean, her hair blowing wild in the wind, her
mischievous eyes twinkling in the golden sun.

And many thanks to Mary May Burruss
My writing teacher and friend.
Your guidance and patience is deeply appreciated.

Contents

Introduction

I grew up in Texas where hunting and fishing were a way of life. My earliest memory is catching a trout in the surf of Port Aransas while my father cheered me on. I spent much of my childhood at my mother's hill country ranch outside of Austin where I learned outdoor skills at an early age. Lakes in the valleys teemed with bass and catfish that fed me when I was a starving student at the University of Texas at Austin. Dove hunting was a Texas tradition each fall when millions of birds migrated south to Mexico. During the hunting season we ate as much dove as beef.

When I was old enough, my father took me hunting in south Texas brush country where the abundance of quail and deer was staggering. He helped me hone my hunting skills and develop a rugged individualism characteristic of the western culture. We always had two or three English Springer Spaniels and other bird dogs around the house. These were working dogs trained to retrieve birds in hot and cold weather. If they couldn't retrieve, there was no need to have them. A dog had to earn his keep.

I discovered duck hunting during college and became an absolute fanatic about this new bird to chase during frigid winters. I learned the attention to detail necessary to be completely camouflaged when stalking animals in their own environment. In one of the stories of this book, I described the hardship and endurance required to match wits with hardy ducks. Without a tough and brilliant retriever, icy duck hunts would not be possible.

When the economy in Texas crashed in the 1980's, I moved to Florida where I turned to fishing as my primary outlet for outdoor life. I knew how to catch freshwater fish, but the lure of saltwater grabbed me and I became an uncompromising offshore fishing fool. I was completely challenged to show the ocean gods that I could take anything they threw at me. Several of these stories recreate memorable storms at sea that took endurance, and not a small amount of luck, to survive. I learned that although I might not catch fish every time I went out, I could count on seeing something new, or having an unexpected adventure on every trip. Hence, the name of my boat was *Boat Tales.*

I was in between boats when my wife, Annie, and I saw that beautiful, twenty-one foot Aquasport walkabout one day. I instantly knew we had to have her, and *Boat Tales* became my second mistress that I absolutely loved. I gave her lots of TLC. In return, she never failed to bring me home, no matter how bad the seas or what I asked of her.

Boat Tales is no longer around, but I considered that model to be the finest small boat ever built for the big ocean. Although many fishermen preferred center consoles, I thought my heavier walkabout was far superior. I could pack all the gear I wanted in the cabin, take three buddies along, put up the plastic curtains, and stay dry and warm in five-foot seas all day long. Can't do that in a center console.

I was consumed with trolling for dolphin, cobia, wahoo, and tuna, just as I had been for duck hunting. I collected the finest rods, reels, and lures. I studied knots and baits until late at night. I put together a crew of similar fanatics, and we tore up the fish.

I took *Boat Tales* to Nassau, Bahamas, where Annie and I lived for two years; ostensibly to work, but really to fish, boat, and chase Jimmy Buffet's elusive dream of island life.

I quickly found that my reels were not big enough for Bahamian fish, so I upgraded to bigger lures and eighty pound reels and line. The big fish and turquoise water inspired me to start writing stories for the first time. I learned why Hemingway went to the islands to write. The complete escape from the rat race of the modern world allowed the right side of my brain to open up for the first time and start writing. Real stories. How did a good old boy from Texas hang a right and end up on a different road? I'm not really sure, but I'm glad I did. Back to fishing and boating.

I met Doctor Greg Neil in Nassau and was immediately attracted to his laid back Jamaican outlook on life. Don't worry, be happy, have some rum. His smile was warm and generosity boundless. We had many adventures in his twenty six-foot World Cat, exploring the gin-clear waters of the Bahamas while his stereo boomed reggae music. He swore his subwoofers attracted fish. We are close friends and share a love of the free spirit of the open sea.

A photo album of pictures to accompany *Boat Tales* can be viewed at www.islandtales.biz. These stories are mostly true, though names have been changed. There are still many island stories to be told, but those can wait for another day.

Gordon England
From the Tiki Bar at Green Parrot Cafe
Nassau, Bahamas

1100 pounds of Albacore Tuna and Dolphin off Baja

55 pound dolphin at Highbourne Cay, Exumas

Bad Storm

The sixty-foot wooden boat dropped fifteen feet straight down through the air, landing flat on its bottom! WHAM!! CRACK!! I waited for the hull to splinter apart and sink, killing all of the men in our family. Dad and I scrambled for life jackets. There was no lifeboat, not that we had a chance to launch one in fifteen-foot seas and load our eleven miserable crewmembers into it. Most of the men on the boat would have gladly welcomed death by drowning anyhow, rather than continue through seasickness on this fishing trip from hell. By some miracle, the boat did not break up. From a valley between towering waves, we watched another fifteen footer crash over us, rolling the boat ninety degrees onto its side. The boat magically popped back up and the captain kept going blindly through the storm. I prayed 'Lord we are in your hands. Please get us back home.'

In April of 1964, Dad had me wound up for my first deep sea fishing trip. He arranged for the men of our family to go on a party boat out of Freeport, Texas, to the snapper banks in the Gulf of Mexico. I was sleepless the

1

week before the trip, imagining giant fish. I was not sure what a red snapper was, but I wanted one. By Friday after school I was raring to go.

The plan was to drive all night to Freeport on Friday, leave the dock at five o'clock Saturday morning, sail fifty miles out to the snapper banks, and spend the day loading up on big red snapper. At least that was the way Dad explained it to me, the only child on the trip.

Dad and I spent the week planning the trip and packing our gear into his station wagon. It was warm for April, but we still drove all over Dallas to find small long-underwear, a rain suit, and rubber boots for me. Being just ten years old, I didn't understand why he was worried about my clothes. I would soon be glad he did.

When Dad got off work Friday, we started our trek southward to the Gulf. We pulled into San Marcos four hours later to pick up Jack and Bud Weiser, Richard Altman, Steve Altman, and Ralph Shultz. We were true landlubbers, this being the first ocean trip for most us. The first order of business was to ice down several cases of beer in the backs of our cars.

The caravan continued an hour southward to San Antonio, where we pick up my grandfather, Adolph Scheh, and his friend Eberhard Weigand, the senior member of the crew at eighty-years old. We left San Antonio and weaved through south Texas on small, dark highways.

Our convoy pulled into Freeport, two hours southwest of Houston, at three-thirty. We descended upon a fisherman's café where we filled up on mountains of eggs and pancakes. You had to fish on a full stomach, right?

After breakfast, we made our way to the docks and boarded the party boat Deep Sea Rider. The interior cabin was lined with bunks and wooden seats along each wall.

Above the bunks were primitive sliding glass windows. Under the cockpit was a head accessed by a ladder. At the stern was a large deck with ice chests for mountains of beer and fish. Two mates from the boat helped us load our gear. We were ready, but the Captain had not shown up yet. Not to worry, the guys were not about to let a late captain cut in on the fun. They launched a serious poker game and kept drinking beer.

Soon Captain Jim staggered down the pier and jumped on the boat. He stumbled into the cabin, fell flat on his face, and passed out cold in the middle of the aisle. Everybody roared with laughter and returned to the poker game. The mates threw Captain Jim onto a bunk, fired up the engines, and sailed out the harbor alongside her sister ship into the black Gulf. Exhausted from a long night, I crawled into a bunk and fell asleep dreaming of big fish.

In those days, there were no weather channels, radar for storm predictions, or satellite photographs. Fishermen were true sailors, navigating with just a radio, compass, and map. Our trip was supposed to be was an easy three-hour cruise to the snapper grounds; what we didn't know that fateful day was that a fierce storm awaited us in the Gulf.

As the dawn turned grey an hour later, I awoke to four-foot waves throwing the boat around. The poker game and beer drinking was over and the guys were watching the seas with concern. Captain Jim awakened, staggered to his feet, and declared "Don't worry none about these waves boys, Deep Sea Rider is a sturdy boat. We're gonna clean up on snapper today!" The response was timid from our novices who had not been at sea before.

The sun briefly peeked above the sea, revealing an endless sight of what to us were tall waves. The sky darkened again as huge raindrops spattered from rolling clouds. Winds turned hard and frigid as waves steepened from long rollers to short rockers. The guys laughed at Dad and me when we donned our warm, dry clothes and rubber boots, though I now saw Dad's wisdom in bringing bad weather gear. Most of our buddies just wore T-shirts and looked enviously at us when cold rain started falling. Those with weak stomachs soon turned green and headed to their bunks.

Our large boat was still handling the five-foot waves pretty well. Heavy rain seeped through the sliding glass windows, soaking the bunks. Though it was difficult to sleep, there was little else to do. By now, most men had dropped into the bunks like flies. Beer and eggs made a second appearance as guys staggered to the head in the bow or out to the stern to chum over the rail, but not good old Uncle Steve.

He proclaimed, "I'ya sailed all over the Pacific in the navy during the big war and I never once got sick. I'm not startin' now," slamming down another beer while singing navy songs.

Two hours later Captain Jim announced we reached the snapper grounds. The seas were treacherous at ten feet high; about the scariest site most of us had ever seen. It was miserable cold and rain came down in heavy sheets. Nobody had any interest in fishing.

Captain Jim struggled with navigation because the compass rocked too much to take a reading. Most of the guys were in advanced stages of God-pleez-let-me-die seasickness. Jack and Ralph lay together in one bunk, sick as dogs. They could no longer stagger to the head. They just hung their heads over the side of the bunks and threw up in the aisles.

Jack begged the Captain, "Paleez turn around and take us back. I gots a hundred dollar bill says you can get us back to port." When Ralph rolled over and spewed all over Jack, my young mind went into shock. I'd never seen people throw up on each other.

Captain Jim replied, "I'll try to find calmer water where we can fish."

I asked Dad, "When are we going back?" He grimly shook his head and held on to the railing while the boat tossed violently.

We had a problem in that Steve kept drinking beer, but the beer was back in the stern. There was no way he or anybody else could walk back there in ten feet seas to get more beer. A powwow was held among the adults.

Dad turned to me. "Gordon, it's your job to retrieve beer for Steve. If he tries to go out back he'll fall overboard."

He tied a line around my waist and sent me after beer. We were too shocked to think about a life jacket for me. I crawled to the back of the boat on my hands and knees through the cold rain and wildly pitching floor, opened the cooler, pulled out a beer in each hand, and laid down on my back on the floor. Dad pulled the line and slid me back to the cabin. When I reached the cabin I staggered through the aisles sloshing with swill and proudly handed Steve his beer.

An hour later he bellowed, "More beer."

I looked at Dad. He nodded. I tied on the line and crawled out for more beer.

Around ten o'clock Jack pleaded, "Captain you gotta take us back."

"We got a problem boys. I don't know where we are or which way to go. We gotta ride out this storm."

The waves had grown to twelve feet, bouncing the boat too violently to read the compass. We were out of radio range of anybody but our sister ship, who was also lost. Not that it really mattered. The only safe direction Captain Jim could steer was straight into the waves. Attempting any other course would have swamped us.

All I saw through the windows was a wall of rain and mountainous waves previously inconceivable to me. The heavy rain was horizontal, pouring through the windows and doors, soaking everyone to the bone except Dad and me bundled up in cold weather gear.

Deep Sea Rider struggled up the front side of a wave, teetered to a stop at the crest, then barreled down the backside to the trough below, burying the bow into the water as the next wave crashed over the top of the boat. Captain Jim struggled with the wheel, straightened us out, and started up the next roller coaster wave. Again and again. Numb with exhaustion and fear I wondered if this boat ride would ever end. To keep from being thrown around the boat, I kept a death grip on the bunk poles until my hands cramped closed. Noon came and went.

Now Jack was begging Captain Jim, "I'll make it $300 to take us back now!"

"I would, but I don't know where back is."

The blinding rain, washing-machine ocean, lightening flashes, and dark clouds continued endlessly. The waves were now fifteen feet high, roaring through at ten-second intervals to crash onto the top of the boat, over and over for hours. The sick guys in the bunks no longer lifted their heads over the edge of the bunks. They just lay in their bunks holding on for dear life. A good two to three inches of slop sloshed up and down the floor of the cabin.

Steve still drank beer, sending me out to the stern to fetch more. When he became hungry he ate sausage and sardines. At one point he fell off the bunk, dropped a sardine on the floor in the pink slop, picked it up, and ate it with a big grin. Dad and I had resisted sickness up to that point, but Steve's show finally caused us to hang our heads over the bunk and chum. With the boat being tossed around like a cork, Steve was constantly thrown from his seat, landing in the slush, crawling back up into his seat, and falling back down again screaming and laughing.

Later that afternoon Steve went to the wildly pitching head in the bow. After a while we noticed he had not come out, but we heard him yelling over the roar of the storm. When Dad opened the head door I wanted to laugh, but it hurt too much. Steve was being thrown all over the tiny room with his pants down around his ankles like handcuffs.

He was trapped in the hold, yelling and screaming, "Get me outta here."

Why he did not break any bones was beyond me. The good lord really watched over him. Dad and the mate climbed down into the cramped head. At that moment the boat crashed into the bottom of another wave, tossing Dad and the mate on top of Steve. Screaming and yelling, they dragged Steve out of the head and threw him back in his seat.

He laughed then turned to me, "Gimme another beer, Gordon."

I tied the rope on and crawled across the bucking deck again to retrieve beer while angry waves crashed over me. If not for the rope I would have been washed overboard to a dark horrible death. Dad pulled me back through the ten feet of eternity to the safety of the cabin. Too sick and scared to say a word, I staggered up the aisle and bounced off the bunks until I reached Steve. He laughed, took the beer, and popped the top.

Captain Jim was hopelessly lost in survival mode as he valiantly fought to keep control of the boat. Over and over we dropped off the fifteen-foot waves, crashing down into freezing water that deluged the boat. Each time I thought we were goners. Too scared and too sick to pray, I just held on to the bunk for what seemed line an eternity.

Most of the guys were passed out by now. They were soaked, frozen, blue, and did not move or respond to us. For all I knew they were dead. Each crash of the boat caused them to fly up from the bunk and smash into the ceiling while slosh from the aisles splashed over everyone.

Late in the afternoon the storm finally laid down, enabling Captain Jim to read the compass and take a heading back to port. The waves were still eight to ten feet high when night descended on us. Captain Jim couldn't see the approaching waves in the dark, often hitting them at the wrong speed and angles, throwing us around like ping-pong balls. The night was pitch black. The only thing I could see was the light of the dashboard. Every time we raced down the face of a wave I thought we were descending into the gaping mouth of hell.

We miraculously made our way back to port about eleven o'clock that night. While we had motored out to the snapper banks in three hours, it took fifteen tortuous hours to find our way back. By then Jack had come back to life and was only offering Captain Jim fifty dollars to get us back. And wouldn't you know it, Steve was still drinking beer.

We were shell-shocked, drowned rats when we stepped onto the dock. To a man we had thought we were going down at any one of a dozen terrible times when waves crashed over the boat. Our sister ship had broken up during the storm and gone down with no survivors. The big sailor in the sky was watching over us for sure that incredible day.

Perseverance

Gordon and Annie with 52-pound cobia
that won FSFA Cobia Tournament

Cold Duck

My wife and I watched the big ball on Time Square drop at midnight with a group of friends. She saw me glance out the window at the hard blowing north wind.

When I turned back to the party, she simply said, "Are you going?"

I smiled. "Of course. The forecast is for rain turning to sleet and ice by daylight. You know the only thing cold is good for is duck hunting and snuggling."

"I'll put the coffee on."

"Thanks, I knew you would understand."

A few minutes later I called Ronnie Kirkwood, "Are you still up?"

"Off course. Isn't this perfect weather?"

"I'll pick you up at four thirty. See if your brother wants to come along, if he's not too drunk."

Duck hunting is a masochistic sport undertaken by the hardy or foolish in the most miserable of winter conditions. If the north wind is not blowing at twenty miles an hour, temperature hovering around freezing, and rain turning to sleet, ducks will not be flying much and

11

crazy duck hunters will not be crawling through the mud an hour before sunrise telling themselves they are having fun, damn it.

An hour later I had packed my camouflaged Remington 870 long barrel three inch magnum shotgun, boxes of No. 4 magnum shells, a duck call, dog whistle, flashlight, and two dozen teal and mallard decoys in camo bags. I prepared for the cold by laying out extra insulated clothes, a heavy waterproof jacket, and waders.

Brewster, my brown and white English Springer Spaniel, watched me and anxiously whined. Springers were wonderful hunting dogs, oblivious to cold weather, making them perfect dogs for duck hunting in the dead of winter. When I finished gathering the gear, he lay down on the shotgun to prevent me from leaving without him.

"Don't worry old pal. I wouldn't dream of going without you." He raised his head and panted with excitement. "Let's try to get a little bit of sleep."

I tossed and turned, waiting for the alarm to go off at 3:30. When I climbed out of bed, Brewster walked to the door and sat in front of it to prevent me from escaping. After a quick breakfast, I loaded up the station wagon and headed to Ronnie's house through gusty wind and rain. When I pulled into the driveway, I saw frosty breath from Ronnie and Steve waiting in the garage.

Ronnie asked, "Are you ready to slay some ducks?"

"You betcha. We'll limit out today. This is perfect weather, twenty-eight degrees and falling. Climb on in guys."

We filled up the back of the station wagon with gear and headed north to Kyle with the heater on high. Brewster was in his cage whining with anticipation. The further north we went, the more the temperature dropped. Rain turned to sleet, then ice.

I had the perfect ten-acre duck lake in Kyle, Texas, thirty-miles south of Austin on my family ranch. By the time we arrived there, the wipers were losing the battle to keep ice off the windshield. When we stopped to unlock the gate in the headlights of the car, I let Brewster out to run the last mile and wear off some energy.

Even though the road was gravel, the car slipped through icy water. Through the dark I carefully drove to the back of the duck lake's dam.

I said, "Here we go guys. Lets get geared up."

We opened the doors to be met by a blast of wickedly cold wind and snow.

Ronnie shivered, "I don't think this wind has slowed down since it left Canada. There's nothing but telephone poles and barbed wire between here and there."

Steve replied, "Jesus, I hear you."

I laughed, "Let's go, you wimps."

We laboriously turned on electric socks, climbed into waders, buttoned up jackets, loaded shells into coat pockets, put on face masks, and donned two sets of gloves. Bogged down with enough clothes to be an astronaut, I could not swing the large bundle of decoys onto my back.

"Steve, help me out. Hold up these decoys while I get into the shoulder straps."

After Steve helped Ronnie and I with the decoy bags, we carefully picked up our shotguns. We turned on our flashlights and headed into the dark.

"Brewster, heel up" I ordered. I didn't want him to run over the dam and scare away any ducks in the lake. He obediently fell in behind me.

With the top-heavy backpack of decoys I felt like an arctic explorer. I took slow, careful steps on the slippery ground. I knew if I fell down I would need help to get back up. We climbed to the top of the forty-foot high east-to-west dam. The reflection of water was barely visible through the snow and wind. We walked down the front of the dam in knee high brown grass lightly crusted in snow. The north wind was blocked by the dam, which made for smooth water at the edge of the lake.

My flashlight picked up the duck blind ten feet from the lake. This was no ordinary duck blind. This was my one of a kind, first class duck blind like no others. Ronnie and I had sunk a ten-foot diameter aluminum corn silo into a pit next to the lake, leaving only the two feet above ground. We camouflaged the silo with paint, surrounded it with brush, and put in a wood floor to keep us above water and mud. A section of the top of the silo was hinged, so we could raise the lid to jump up and shoot. Inside the blind were a bench and small shelf along the front to hold shells, coffee, and duck calls. Behind the bench were additional decoys and a propane heater for mornings like this. After we unloaded our gear, we walked to the water.

Steve exclaimed, "You won't believe this. The lake's frozen!" Sure enough, a quarter-inch of ice covered the lake.

"Not to worry guys, Brewster will take care of that."

I threw a stick out onto the ice and commanded, "Fetch."

He charged out, breaking a path through the ice. With his tail wagging, he brought back the stick and dropped it at my feet to play the game again. After three more trips, he had created a twenty-foot hole in the ice.

14

"This is just what we want guys," I said through chattering teeth. "This is the only wind protected open water for miles. The ducks will be swarming to get in here soon. Lets hurry up and get the dekes out before sunrise."

With heavy gloves on, we clumsily unwrapped the weights and lines from the decoys. Brewster anxiously watched as we threw them out to the hole in the water.

When one of the decoys landed upside down, "Fetch," was all I had to say. Off he dashed through the water to retrieve the upside down decoy, leaving the others alone.

"Good boy." The years I spent training him sure paid off. He sat down shivering as ice forming in his fur. He watched to make sure the rest of the decoys were right side up. He loved this game.

We threw out the remaining decoys in a strategic J pattern that invited ducks to sit down in open water fifteen-yards from our blind. The first glimpses of light slipped through purple, angry clouds. We had located the blind so that sunrise was to our backs, making it difficult for the ducks to see us. With no wind behind the dam, dancing snowflakes built up lightly on the tall weeds, not yet heavy enough to crush them down. We trudged back to the blind and hid under the roof to stay dry. By now Brewster was covered with ice. He ran around in circles, dug holes to stay warm, and then ran around again while he waited for ducks.

I called, "Come back here."

He pushed through the small hinged door on the side of the blind and slipped in. He shook violently, sending ice and mud flying all over us, then laid down close to the gas heater.

Looking through darkness over the water, I saw fleeting shadows of teal slip through the cold grey dawn. They were gone before we could raise a gun. A few more minutes, then it was light enough to shoot.

Ronnie whispered excitedly, "Six widgeons at ten o'clock."

Steve replied, "Wait until they land."

The formation of birds swooped down over us, lifted up to make one more inspection circle, and then dropped down to land into the wind. They were at twenty-five yards, outside the open water that had been cleared by Brewster. When the white and green-headed widgeons dropped their legs to land, they hit the slick ice and tumbled onto their backs, spinning like hockey pucks. We laughed so hard we decided not to shoot them. The widgeons got to their feet, looking around sheepishly. They shook all over, straightened out their feathers, and flew away to find a better lake.

A few minutes later Steve whispered, "I got a flock of mallards at nine o'clock. Keep your heads down."

This was great because I was best at left-to-right shots. With anticipation I pushed the safety off my shotgun and turned my face down. I resisted the urge to look up, which would have scared the ducks like a big red flag. We watched out of the corner of our eyes until the ducks set their wings at twenty yards to land in the open water.

I hissed, "Now!"

We jumped up and fired, catching the mallards six inches above the water with wings open and bellies exposed. I tumbled the lead duck with a single shot, while Ronnie and Steve each also took a bird. Brewster dashed through the door, hitting the water in two leaps. Dead ducks still rocked in the water as he swam through the decoys and grabbed the first mallard. He came back, tail wagging, and barking excitedly with a large duck in his mouth.

"Good boy." He dropped the duck at my feet, then eagerly plunged back into the lake to retrieve more birds. By the time Brewster made two more trips, ice balls looked like white cockle burrs in his thick, brown hair. When he dropped the last bird, he shivered with cold, but looked up at us with tail wagging expectantly.

His eager eyes said, "Hurry up and shoot more ducks, Dad. I'm ready."

Despite all of my insulated clothes, I was bitter cold. Just looking at my dog made it worse. Ice formed on the outside of my facemask where my breath came through and snow covered my hat.

Ronnie laughed, "You look like Frosty the snowman."

"I feel like Frosty's snowballs." My numb fingers could barely handle the shotgun, much less push the safety and pull the trigger.

Steve kidded, "You're a wimp."

"And a damned cold wimp at that. I lost feeling in my toes thirty minutes ago. How about you?"

Steve jabbed, "What toes? I thought they fell off already. Can't you turn that heater up any more?"

"It is supposed to heat a small room, not the great outdoors," I replied with a shaking voice.

Fifteen minutes later a flock of twelve bluebills circled over the lake. I blew my duck call, coaxing them closer.

"Let them land," I whispered. "See how close we can get them to the blind."

The small black ducks made one more pass and then landed in a tight group in open space between decoys. I brought my shotgun to my shoulder and fired into the middle of the flock. Only three of the bluebills rose off the water. Ronnie and Steve dispatched those three while I shot at the wounded birds that tried to swim away.

Brewster bounded out the door and into the chaos of ducks everywhere. Six of the twelve birds were still alive, flopping around in the midst of decoys. Brewster plunged into the water, retrieving live ducks first. We shot the wounded birds so they wouldn't escape under the ice.

Brewster dove into the water repeatedly retrieving ducks for the next fifteen minutes. He was really cold, shaking, and whining, but wouldn't stop. A couple of the decoy lines became entangled around him, slowing him down when he came ashore. After I cleared the lines he turned around and jumped back in the water.

"Good boy. Fetch the next one," I sure was glad I was not wading out through the ice myself.

My amazing dog retrieved duck after duck through the ice and frigid water. When one of the wounded ducks attempted to escape across the ice, he chased it by crashing though the thin ice with his large feet. We cheered when he caught the bird. With his soft mouth, the bird was still alive after Brewster retrieved it.

I sent him out again for the last live duck. When the duck dove under the water, Brewster swam in circles for five minutes, but that duck never came back up. I had been told that some ducks dive to the bottom and hold onto the grass to drown themselves rather than be caught. Now I believed it.

I called the dog, "Come back here. Let's get warmed up." Back to the blind we went, three shivering guys and one shaking dog huddled around the heater.

After we warmed up a little I said, "I've had enough fun guys. Let's pack it up."

I sent Brewster out to retrieve decoys this time.

18

I commanded, "Fetch." He looked at me with *No ducks Dad* on his ice covered face.

I picked up a rock and threw it at the decoys, again ordering "Fetch." Brewster reluctantly swam out and brought back a decoy.

"Good boy. Now go get the rest of them. The water's too deep for us."

He barked and then went back out for the other twenty-three decoys, one at a time. Despite being completely water logged, covered with ice, and whining with misery, he went back time after time until all of the decoys were retrieved.

By then we were also soaked from wet ducks and decoys. We shouldered the birds and waterlogged gear, then drudged back to the car in slow motion through snow and ice. Brewster waited for us, anxious to get into the warm car. We slowly drove back through the mud and slippery roads.

Ronnie said, "Gordon. That dog of yours is unbelievable. No way we could've hunted without him."

I smiled, "That's the best duck hunting dog I have ever had. Wanna come back tomorrow?"

They rolled their eyes, hesitated, and then said, "Count us in."

Gordon and Tom Black with mallard and Canadian goose

The Other Side

Gordon asked Annie, "Guess where we're going Saturday."

"Tell me."

"Fishing on Ron Sparks' new thirty-six foot Delta, the Perseverance. We're going to the other-side."

"The other side of what?"

"The other side of the Gulf Stream. Yellowfin, bonita, and skipjack tuna stay sixty to a hundred miles offshore. Only the big boats go after them because you gotta have lots of gas and be able to handle big seas on this trip."

"Who's going with us?"

"Lou Ziazas and his son, Troy. Lou's been fishing for years on his own boat. He's gonna train us rookies."

"Wow, this will be a big adventure. I'll start planning the food. I can make lots of sandwiches," Annie said with a big smile.

When Annie and Gordon showed up at Harbor Town Marina in Port Canaveral at three o'clock Saturday morning, Ron already had the engines warmed up.

Gordon shouted, "Ahoy!" Ron climbed out of the engine compartment.

"Come aboard and look at these new twin Caterpillar 3208's."

Gordon looked under the hatch and exclaimed, "They're gorgeous. The whole engine room is spotless. I'd expected nothing less from an engineer like you."

"Lou, show them where to stow their gear."

Annie said, "I brought plenty of food."

Lou replied, "I'm glad you came along. There's a refrigerator down in the cabin."

"I'll go down below and organize the galley."

A long distance run to the other-side required more gear and supplies than a normal fishing trip. Gordon helped stow ten bags of ice, six twelve-packs of frozen ballyhoo, four rods with gold Penn International 50 reels, and a bucket full of trolling lures.

At three-thirty Ron ordered, "Cast the lines. We got an appointment with tuna at daybreak. Can't be late."

When Lou pushed Perseverance away from the dock, we were the only boat moving in the darkness. Ron idled smooth as a ghost through still waters of the port. Our wavelets rippled quietly into boats and seawalls. Familiar smells of salt, shrimp boats, and diesel wafted across the water, triggering deep memories from Gordon's past fishing journeys. He wondered what today would hold.

Once past the port's entrance, Ron turned eastward and pushed the boat up to cruising speed of twenty-one knots. The deep bow cut through the glassy ocean like butter. Gordon and Annie climbed the ladder from the deck up to the dark flybridge where Ron sat at the wheel. His console had a few lit gauges and an early model Loran with a numeric screen. Gordon noted there were no directional electronics or lit compass on the dash.

He asked, "How do you know where you're going?"

"We just head east until we find fish. To come back we head west, can't miss Florida. I didn't have time to activate the light on the compass, but don't worry, once the sun comes up we can see it." Gordon glanced sideways at Annie with raised eyebrows.

He asked, "How do you know where we are?"

"From the latitude and longitude on the loran I can find where we are on the chart. I know the coordinates for the port, so I can steer my way back, no problem."

"You're kidding. You calculate the course by watching the lat longs change?"

"Long numbers are east-west and latitude numbers are north-south. I've been doing that for years. We're in the shipping lanes, so help me watch for other boats. They're supposed to have their lights on, but you never know."

Gordon turned to Annie, "At this speed we couldn't see a dark boat until we hit it. This night running is spooky business. Oh the heck with it. We're having fun now."

He asked, "How long does it take to get to the other-side?"

"We'll have a three hour run. Why don't you go help Lou rig lures? Annie, stay up here and help me watch for boats. Be sure to give me plenty of warning if you see anything."

Gordon laughed. "Yeah Annie, give Ron plenty of warning." He climbed down the ladder to join the rest of the crew.

An hour later a color change of the water and two-foot ripples indicated they had entered the Gulf Stream. Two-foot waves were no match for the superbly designed hull of Perseverance. Ron continued eastward another two hours while the crew rigged baits, lines, rods, and saved energy for big action. Since Gordon and Troy were too excited to sleep, Lou primed them about fast tuna action.

"We'll be running and gunning at high speed all day. Tuna chase schools of pilchards, so we watch for swarms of birds scavenging pieces of bait left by tuna. We'll drag ballyhoo with skirts. When we see birds, we speed up ahead of the school and then slow down to let them intercept our lures. Bonita run five to ten pounds, but yellowfins get up to one hundred pounds or more. They're the hardest fighting fish in the sea. Are you ready?"

Gordon replied, "I was born ready. You just find the fish."

Annie went below and soon emerged with coffee and doughnuts as the faint light of sunrise peeked through black night ahead of us.

She announced, "You better eat now, we'll be fishing soon."

Gordon looked at Lou. "Annie's gonna keep us well fed today."

The sun broke the edge of the sea in a thin, gold sliver, revealing the sea flattened out smooth as glass.

Ron yelled to the crew, "Okay guys. We just left the Gulf Stream. Lou, you got everything ready?"

"Aye-aye Captain. Rods are rigged and bait is ready. Troy, go up in the tuna tower and look for birds."

Ron zigzagged eastward at sixteen knots to maximize coverage of the ocean.

An hour later we heard Troy yell, "Birds at ten o'clock." Ron turned the boat toward a flock of birds a half-mile away and the fire drill started. A melee of fifty plus white terns swirled and dove on baitfish that jumped out of the water to escape murderous tuna attacking from below. Yellowfins jumped completely out of the water to catch fleeing pilchards in midair. The awesome frenzy of fish, birds, and pilchards moved at fifteen knots.

Ron sped up to twenty knots on a parallel course. When he pulled ahead of the school, baits were dropped in front of a riot of fish and birds. He backed off the throttle, allowing the fish to catch up to the lures. The crew braced for battle. Thrashing fish approached the lures, sensed the boat, and turned left, ignoring the baits. Ron sped ahead of the school again, swerved left, and slowed down. The tuna spooked again and disappeared into deep blue water.

Ron circled for fifteen minutes, then spotted the birds a mile to the northeast. He raced in, but the fish sounded before baits were even put in the water.

This set the pattern for the remainder of the day. Run at high-speed north and east until birds were sighted, race after them, make one or two passes through the fish with the lures, no bites, and then the fish would sound without touching the baits. By three o'clock the crew was tired of chasing fish with lockjaw.

Lou asked Ron, "How far out are we?"

"Just a minute, let me calculate. Hmmm. About eighty miles."

"And how far north?"

"Hmmm. We're off New Smyrna Beach."

Lou replied, "We gotta long run back home. I've had all the fun I can stand. What do you say we head back guys? I

25

see clouds building in the west." Ron agreed and turned southwest.

Five minutes later Gordon shouted, "Birds at two o'clock."

Ron steered toward the swarm of birds while the crew grabbed rods and dropped baits one more time. When the lures passed through the school of fish, the shotgun line received a powerful hit that bent the heavy rod almost double. Gordon reached to the overhead rocket launcher and struggled to remove the bucking rod. He jammed the rod butt into his stomach and watched line screamed off the reel. This was Gordon's first large fish and he didn't know how much abuse his reel could take before it melted.

Lou yelled, "That's a big fish. He hasn't slowed down yet. Troy, get a fighting belt for Gordon. Ron, chase that fish before he spools the reel." The rest of the crew quickly reeled in the other lines while Gordon waited for the run to stop before he tightened the drag and cranked on the reel. Ron turned the boat and slowly gained on the tuna while Gordon struggled to reel line.

Lou commanded, "Don't pump with your arms, use your legs and back. Tighten up the drag a bit."

"I can't stop him, he's huge." Gordon sat on the ice chest and braced his feet against the rail while the tuna dove deep, taking out more line.

He complained, "Ron, you need a fighting chair in this boat. God this is a big fish."

"Keep reeling, unless you want Troy to take the rod."

"No way. That's my fish."

Gordon pumped and reeled, pumped and reeled, gaining line back inches at a time. Every time the tuna changed direction the ice chest slid across the deck and slammed Gordon into the opposite rail. After thirty minutes, his arms and back were wracked with cramps and his hands were locked into claws. He reeled by moving his arms up and down. He was more exhausted than he had ever been, but was not about to give up. Annie poured cold water on his face and offered words of encouragement.

Lou yelled, "Don't stop reeling," every time Gordon slowed to rest. To keep the tuna from circling the boat, Ron motored forward at three knots, adding more pull to the line.

Lou exclaimed, "I see color. He's coming up. Stand over here to the port side where I can gaff in front of you. Troy, open the fish box."

Gordon grunted, rose off the ice chest, and staggered to the rail. At last he saw the fish causing him so much pain. The amazing beast was five feet long, over one hundred pounds. Yellow pectoral fins extended twelve inches on each side. A powerful tail pulsated from side to side.

Troy said, "Pull him in closer."

"I'm trying, but my arms are killing me."

"Keep reeling, he's almost here. Ron, a little more to the left."

Gordon struggled to bring the fish into range of the gaff. The fish rolled onto its side, looking up defiantly with a large black eye. Lou slammed the six-foot metal gaff into the tuna and attempted to lift it into the boat. That's when he realized he had underestimated the size and strength of the fish. The tuna exploded in fury, shaking its head back and forth in a frenzy that pulled Lou downward. Lou grunted and tried to lift again, but the fish was too heavy. The gaff shook violently and broke free from Lou's hands. The end of the gaff now whipped back and forth, severely pounding Lou's arms. He howled and jumped back. The tuna dove under the boat. Gordon was jerked down, his rod near the water. When the gaff disappeared into the frothing sea, the line broke free, causing Gordon to tumble backwards.

Whack whack whack. A loud noise came from the bottom of the boat.

Lou screamed, "Stop."

Ron killed the engines to stop the dreadful noise. Blood boiled up from the stern. The crew stared at each other in disbelief. Lou was really pissed and hurt.

He moaned, "I couldn't hold on. The gaff beat me up."

Ron asked, "Are your arms broken?"

"No. But they hurt like hell."

Annie anxiously asked, "What was all that noise?"

Ron replied, "I don't know, but it wasn't good."

"What are we going to do?"

"Troy, go into the locker in the galley. See if you can find a mask and snorkel. Lets clear the deck so I can go overboard to see what the problem is."

The crew stared at each other in disbelief. The adrenaline of the long fight still prevented clear thought. Broken down at eighty miles out. This was no longer fun.

Troy climbed out of the cabin and reported, "I found two masks and a snorkel." He looked over the stern, "Do you have a dive ladder?"

Ron replied, "No, but there's a dive platform."

"Oh."

Ron put on a mask and snorkel and stepped over the transom onto the dive platform.

"I'll go underneath and check the prop."

The slick ocean of the morning had changed to three feet seas with the advancing clouds. The stilled boat swung crossways to the waves, rocking back and forth.

Ron dove under the boat while Gordon sat down in exhaustion and stared at Annie.

She nervously said, "I can't believe he dove into all that blood. There's gonna be sharks." *Jaws* had given her a deep terror of sharks.

Gordon said, "Your job is to watch for sharks while we fix the boat."

Annie's took her post at the stern. With wide eyes she stared into the bottomless blue water for approaching fins. Ron popped out of the water and crawled up onto the dive platform.

Troy asked, "What did you see?"

"We have a problem. The gaff is wrapped around the port drive shaft and the line and wire leader is wrapped all around the propeller. Of course, the fish is gone."

The crew was stunned. Not only had they lost the fish, the fish had crippled the boat.

"We gotta clear this mess or limp home on one motor at slow speed. Troy, go down below and find my toolbox. I need the wire cutters so I can get the wire off the prop. Lou, come help me under the boat."

When Troy brought the wire cutters, Lou put on a mask and joined Ron in the water to dive under the bobbing boat. Thirty-seconds later they surfaced and placed a handful of line on the platform. Down they went again. And again. Each time removing more wire and line from the prop. Each dive under the boat was shorter as they quickly tired out. After ten minutes, they climbed back on the platform and into the boat. They sat for a minute to regain their strength.

Gordon asked, "How's it look?"

Ron replied, "We got all the line and wire off. Now we gotta get the gaff off the drive shaft. Hand me the big pliers. I don't want this damn snorkel. I can't breath when the waves break over it."

They climbed back overboard and dove under the boat. After a minute, they surfaced, grabbed the rocking platform, caught their breath, and went back down again while Annie continued her vigil for sharks. Several dives later they came back up and struggled onto the platform. Bleak looks on their faces foretold more problems.

Ron caught his breath and said, "When I grab the gaff with the pliers, it just spins. Gordon, give us the pipe wrench. Troy, you hold the gaff with the pipe wrench and I'll try to break it off with the pliers." Gordon handed the five-pound wrench to Troy. Back down under the boat went Ron and Troy.

Gordon told Annie, "That's gotta be tough. When I scuba dive with five pounds of weights I sink to the bottom."

She grimly shook her head as she watched for sharks. They surfaced twenty seconds later, gasped for air, then went back down again. When they came back up the next time they threw the pliers, pipe wrench, and a two foot piece of the crooked, one-inch diameter gaff onto the platform. They struggled back on board exhausted.

After a few minutes of hard breathing, Ron said, "Even with both tools, the gaff spins. I can't do this any more. Is there a hacksaw in the tool box?"

Gordon looked in the box and replied, "No."

"Go down in the engine compartment and see if you can find a hack saw." Gordon searched the engine room and the cabin. No hack saw.

Ron dejectedly said, "Okay Lou, see what you can do."

Lou dove into the water and spent the next ten minutes going under for thirty seconds, coming back up for air, then disappearing under the boat again. He finally dragged himself onto the platform, laboring for breath.

He shook his head and gasped, "I loosened it up some, but I can't break it off."

Ron looked at Gordon. "Your turn."

Annie gave Gordon a pained look when he put on the mask and jumped overboard. He looked down into an endless, deep blue abyss streaked with silver rays of sunlight. He saw at least one hundred feet down into nothing. Visions of sharks or some unimaginable creature rising from the depths struck a primordial fear in his mind. He raised his head above the surface and grabbed a breath, deciding not to look down again.

Gordon dove under the boat, grabbed the propeller, and pulled himself toward the inboard drive shaft. The bottom of the boat moved up and down three feet every few seconds. He saw the gold gaff spiraled around the shaft like spaghetti. When he grabbed it and pulled, it just spun in a circle. He pulled again. Nothing.

Gordon kicked back to the surface, took a couple of breaths of air, and dove back under the boat. He turned upside down, placed his feet against the bottom of the bucking boat, and pulled down on the end of the gaff. The shaft had a weak spot where it creased twelve inches from the end. The end of the gaff moved out an inch, straightening at the crease. The boat rose and slammed back down, causing Gordon's feet to slip. The boat banged his hip. When he yelled in pain, his air bubbled out. He pushed away, rose to the surface, and swam to the dive platform. He held on for a minute to catch his breath and then repeated the drill. He braced his feet on the bottom of the boat again and gave a big pull, breaking off the end of the gaff at the crease. He swam back to the surface and handed the foot long piece of gaff to Annie. Gordon was really exhausted. He held onto the bouncing platform, struggling for breath. After two more dives under the boat, he could dive no more. He crawled onto the platform and lay there for a minute to rest. Lou gave him a hand and pulled him back into the boat.

Ron asked, "What does it look like?"

Gordon replied haltingly, "I loosened it a bit more, but there's still three-feet of gaff wound loosely around the shaft. That's all I can do."

The exhausted crew pondered the situation grimly. They had struggled with the gaff for an hour. No one had the energy to dive under the boat again. It was now six o'clock. Dark clouds were building in the west.

Lou asked Ron, "Can you reach anyone on the radio?"

"No, we're too far out."

"Why don't you start the engines and see what happens."

"Good idea."

Ron turned on the motors and gently placed both engines into gear. Everyone held their breath. No knocking. He increased the rpms. Nothing. He increased speed to ten knots. Nothing. At fifteen knots and they heard a light tap of the gaff hitting the bottom of the boat. He backed off the throttle slightly until the tapping stopped.

With a grin Ron said, "I think we're going to be okay."

The crew breathed a big sigh of relief; glad they were not going to spend the night on the boat waiting to be rescued. Ron turned southwest toward the port. Annie went to the cabin and emerged shortly with sandwiches for the worn out crew.

32

It was seven o'clock when they approached a wall of black clouds stretching far to the south. The seas had built to five feet, limiting speed to ten knots into the waves. Ron had no choice but to push through the storm toward home. Rough waves made it impossible to stay in the cabin, so Annie and Gordon sat on two seats on the flybridge next to the captain's chair. Lou and Troy stood on the deck and held onto rails, struggling for balance with each rolling wave. Dark clouds brought an early sunset. A while later, Ron turned the boat and drove slowly downwind for a brief smooth ride.

He told Lou, "Secure the cabin, it's going to be a long night. Bring out the life jackets and spread them on the deck to make a bed to lie on. Troy, look in the drawer under the bunk and find a flashlight. We'll need that for navigating. Anybody needs a pit stop, now is the time. Annie, if you got any coffee left? I sure could use some."

Annie brought him coffee and asked, "How far out are we?"

Ron paused, looked at the loran, and made a mental calculation. "About forty miles."

The crew looked at each other and grimaced. They cleared the deck of rods, rigs, and loose gear, securing the boat for rough riding. Lou, Troy, and Annie lay down on the life jackets.

Gordon climbed up to the flybridge with Ron and reported, "We're ready to go Captain."

Ron replied, "I can navigate roughly with the loran numbers, but the compass is better. You'll have to shine the flashlight on the compass to help me steer the course. The batteries won't last all night, so just turn the flashlight on every few minutes to take a reading."

"Aye aye, captain."

He turned Perseverance around and quartered on a southwest course against the westerly waves. Five-foot waves at four-second intervals took control of the boat, demanding full concentration from Gordon and Ron. Ron worked the dual throttles continuously with his right hand. He accelerated up the face of each wave, then slowed down at the top to avoid racing down the backside and pitchpoling at the bottom. His left hand on the wheel jerked back and forth on the wheel to ensure the boat reached the top of the waves at ninety degrees to avoid being broadsided. Then he steered slightly to the left on the backside of the waves to maintain an average southwesterly heading. At the same time, he watched the loran numbers change and calculated the course heading. The boat bucked violently, preventing Gordon and Ron from sitting in the chairs to operate the controls, so they stood and bent their legs constantly to adjust to the pitching floor. Gordon turned on the flashlight every few minutes to get a compass heading in case Ron's math slipped.

Downstairs, the crew found the only way to lie on the deck was with their feet facing the stern. The life jackets slid toward the back of the boat every time they went up the face of a wave. The crew used their feet to push themselves off the transom. There was also an easterly tailwind that blew noxious diesel fumes back onto deck, causing Annie to feel sick. She periodically staggered up the stairs to get fresh air and calm her stomach.

Nobody slept during this voyage, they just endured. The only saving grace was that no rain fell that night, although the crew was still soaked from waves breaking over the gunnels.

After thirty minutes at the wheel, Ron yelled to Gordon over the noise of the wind and diesels, "Let's switch."

"I don't know how to do this."

"I need a break. I'll show you how."

They waited until they were at the bottom of a wave, then quickly traded places. Gordon grabbed the wheel and adjusted the throttles just as a wave passed under them.

"Whoa. This isn't like driving my little eighteen-footer."

"Watch the tachometers and keep both engines at the same rpm. I'll watch the loran and tell you which direction to steer. Head directly into the waves when they break or we might get rolled."

Gordon grimly settled into a zone, completely concentrating on navigating the boat. Every time Ron turned on the flashlight to check the compass, Gordon's night vision was ruined. Thirty minutes later he was exhausted for the third time that day.

He told Ron, "I gotta quit."

"Okay, give me the wheel and go tell Lou to come up for a while." Gordon climbed down the bouncing stairs and collapsed on the deck.

"Lou, it's your turn. I hope you can read loran numbers."

For the next three and a half hours the crew rotated between driving the boat and lying on the deck sucking noxious diesel fumes. Progress was slow against the Gulf Stream and rough waves. Fatigue set in. The shifts grew shorter. At twenty miles from Port Canaveral, the crew was relieved to see the beam from the Cape Canaveral lighthouse four miles north of the Port. They no longer had to struggle to watch the loran numbers change and hold a course based on the compass.

An hour later Gordon was at the wheel with Lou at his side. Once he passed the lighthouse he planned to make a westerly turn into port, but it seemed the lighthouse was an elusive ghost that stayed in front of them no matter how long they rode.

They rose to the top of a wave and Lou yelled, "Breakers at two o'clock! Turn left!"

They were approaching the Cape Canaveral Shoals at the False Cape, a one to two fathom deep ridge that extended four miles northeast of the tip of the Cape. These shoals were legendary among sailors for sinking ships with massive waves.

Gordon swung the wheel just as a monster wave caught them broadside, throwing the crew across the boat. Perseverance rolled forty-five degrees, then righted herself like a cork.

Ron staggered up the stairs, "What the hell happened?"

Lou pointed, "The shoals!"

Gordon asked Ron, "Can you tell how far offshore we are?"

"No."

"Do you know how far the shoals come out?

"No."

"You take the wheel. I don't want to wreck your boat."

He passed the wheel to Ron as another wave broke over the boat and drenched the crew. They yelled and scrambled to their feet, a surge of adrenaline bringing them of their stupor. They watched the thunderous, white breakers in the dark, fifty yards to starboard. Shallow water caused the ocean's swells to rise up and become very sloppy, tossing the boat like flotsam.

Ron took the wheel and turned the boat southeast, parallel to the breakers. Time after time waves broke over the side of the boat. The crew struggled not to be washed overboard. Gradually Ron pulled away from the shoals.

Gordon yelled, "How do we get back?"

"We go due south until the lighthouse is behind us, then we turn west and follow the buoy line into the port."

"I've been watching that damn lighthouse for hours. I don't think this day will ever end."

"Watch out for more breakers."

"I'm toasted, I'm going to the deck to rest again."

An hour later they finally passed the lighthouse. Ron turned westward at a flashing channel buoy, lining up for the final three miles into rough wind. The waves were no longer five footers. Instead, shallow water caused three-foot chop in all directions. At long last, Perseverance entered calmer waters of the port. However, Ron faced one last challenge of getting the boat into its slip.

Ron ordered, "Lou and Troy, bring out the lines, fenders, and boathooks. I have to turn the boat broadside to the wind and back into the slip. I have only done this in daylight, not in the dark."

Lou asked Ron, "How do I turn on the spreader lights?"

"I don't have them hooked up yet. Gordon and Annie, use the flashlights to guide us in."

Annie looked at Gordon and moaned, "Is this day ever going to end?"

Ron swung the boat around and attempted to back into the slip. A dual engine boat is steered backwards by using the throttles independently, unlike moving forward and steering with the rudder. Increasing the speed of one motor in reverse turns the boat in the opposite direction. The motors pull a boat backwards, causing the front of the boat to swing around like a car having the steering wheel move the rear wheels instead of the front. When Ron pointed the stern at the mouth of the slip and throttled backwards, strong wind pushed the boat sideways past the slip's piling. Gordon's flashlight showed the boat heading right at the piling.

"Stop! Go forward!" Ron shifted the motors into forward and goosed the throttles, jerking the crew across the deck. The boat surged ahead just before hitting the piling. He swung the boat around and tried again. Once again the crosswind pushed the boat out of position. After the long ride, Ron's foggy brain was not working well.

For twenty minutes he repeatedly attempted to bring his boat the last few feet home. Twice he had the boat half way in, only to have the wind twist the boat against the pilings and scrape the sides. The crew was too exhausted to push the boat away from the pilings. Ron pulled back and tried again. After coming so far and so long, the crew watched helplessly, hoping Ron could maneuver Perseverance into the slip and end the trip.

Finally a mate from another boat walked out onto the pier and asked, "You boys need some help?"

"Sure do," replied Lou. "This crosswind's a bitch."

"Throw me a line and I'll guide you in."

With the mate's help they finally brought the boat into the slip and tied it down. The crew stumbled onto the dock in a daze, not believing they were on solid ground. Their twenty-hour ordeal was finally over.

First Marlin

Fathers Day rolled around in Nassau. Reports were coming in of tuna and occasional marlin close to shore and I wanted in on the action. What else would I do but go fishing?

Gary Honkofsky and I launched *Boat Tales* at sunrise from Sandy Port, in western Cable Beach, to catch an early morning bite. Chasing tuna was entirely sight fishing. Summer doldrums had set in to give windless seas. Mirror flat water enabled us to easily see swarming tuna birds and splashing fish at great distances. Once we saw tuna birds, we would rush to the action and fast troll cedar plugs, feathers, and small jet heads through the melee of diving birds and fish crashing on desperate baitfish.

On this morning, we zigzagged northwest at high speed for several hours, but alas, we saw no birds or fish. By ten o'clock we called it a morning and headed back to port. I stopped the boat three miles offshore in 2,000 feet of water to drift and relax for a while. Optimistically, I put a whole squid on an eight-inch cedar plug and on a blue feather jig. We dropped both rigs down fifty feet, put the rods in the holders, and sat back to enjoy the calm turquoise sea and cloudless sky while sipping beer.

A movement on the port side caught my eye. I turned to the stunning sight of a huge marlin surfacing forty-feet away. The last thing I expected to see this close to shore was a marlin. When he gracefully slid under the boat, I saw his back was over two feet wide. Gary and I jumped up, not knowing what to do. Pull in the lines; put out more lines; start trolling; or nothing. For ten seconds we were paralyzed with indecision. We didn't have marlin lures out, and we certainly didn't have heavy gear for fighting a giant fish. All of a sudden the port rod bent over violently, then snapped straight like a spring. Gary pulled in the line and squidless lure. Thirty seconds later the other rod doubled over as line screamed off the Penn 50 International reel loaded with six hundred yards of fifty-pound line. I grabbed the rod and jerked hard several times to set the hook into the bony bill. The marlin realized he was hooked and shifted into high gear. I was almost jerked overboard before Gary grabbed my belt to hold me back. Line screamed off the rod at an unbelievable rate.

I desperately held on to the rod and yelled, "This is the biggest fish I ever hooked. I hope there's enough line on the reel."

Gary asked incredulously "What do we do?" Neither of us knew how to handling a big fish.

I responded, "Clear the deck and get me a rod belt."

Gary strapped a rod belt around my waist. I placed the rod butt in the cup. We looked in awe when the giant marlin jumped twice at two hundred yards creating huge, white splashes, and then took off on another blistering run.

I settled in for a long battle. *I wonder if I have the endurance to catch this beast,* I thought. *I can't stop him on this first run. If I tighten the drag now I risk cutting the line on the fish's bill or tail.*

My normal marlin rig used fifteen feet of two hundred-pound leader to prevent chaffing the line; but today I only had three feet of sixty-pound leader on my light tuna rig. Without a fighting chair on the boat I could only fight this marlin standing up. I had only been at it for a few minutes and my arms were already cramped.

I told Gary, "Break out the fighting harness. I'm not going to last much longer." We looked like clowns as Gary struggled to put the harness around my back while I held onto the rod.

When he finished he asked, "Now what?"

"Get that knee plate and clip it onto the harness."

Once the knee plate was attached I said, "It's hanging too low. Adjust the straps higher." While Gary tried to adjust the straps, I almost lost my grip on the rod twice.

"Now take these side straps and clip them onto the reel." Once the reel was strapped to the harness, I took my cramped hands off the rod. The pull was transferred to my legs and back rather than my aching arms.

By now three hundred yards of line were off the reel and the marlin was still going strong. I hadn't even started reeling. I just hung on, waiting for the marathon run to stop. I watched the knot of the backing line roll off the spool where I had recently spliced on new line.

I yelled, "Start the boat and chase that son of a bitch or he'll spool me." We followed the marlin plowing a big V in the water, but I was still unable to reel in line.

"Faster."

Gary throttled up to fifteen knots before we gained on him. I reeled in one hundred yards of line, inch-by-inch. I was relieved when the backing knot went back on the reel.

We were within fifty yards of the fish when the angle of the line changed. We had gotten too close and spooked the marlin while he was still green. He was sounding.

"Slow down. He's diving."

By now my line was straight down. Gary stopped the boat as the marlin dove with a vengeance. Line once again screamed off the reel, creating that wonderful musical sound of fish and raw strength. Out went the backing knot again. I was not even slowing him down. The power of the fish was unbelievable.

When Gary pulled the gaff out of the fish box, I laughed, "How are you going to gaff a monster marlin with a little six foot dolphin gaff."

He looked at me mystified. "What am I going to do?"

"I don't know. I'll think of something."

"Want me to take the rod?"

"No, this is my fish."

Down and down the fish dove. I still could not reel against the drag. I just held onto the rod waiting to see who would tire first, me or the denizen from the deep.

I thought, *I wish the water wasn't so deep. My line will run out before he reaches the bottom. What the hell am I going to do?* I tightened the drag as much as I dared, to no avail. My back was started to tighten up. We were fifteen minutes into the fight and the marlin had not slowed down a bit. I now understood the stories of marathon struggles with giant marlin that lasted for many hours. What would it to take to slow him down, much less bring this goliath in? I didn't have it in me.

Five hundred yards of line was out when Gary again asked, "What are we going to do?"

"We have two choices. We can tie another rod onto this reel and throw it over board to give us another five hundred yards of line. Or, I can tighten the drag and hope he stops before the knot in the middle breaks. He won't give me enough slack to cut the line and tie it on to another reel."

I thought, *this is a $600 rod and reel. I am not in a high dollar tournament so there is no way I'll throw the rod overboard and sacrifice it to the fish gods.*

The line was down to the last forty yards and the fish was still diving to the bottom of the sea. I tightened the drag all the way down but that did not faze him. When the line got to the end of the spool I put more pressure on the line with my thumb, pulled up hard, and braced for a big surge. The rod jerked down violently then went limp. Gary and I stepped back and looked at each other silently. I slowly reeled in the line with limp arms. Unbelievably, I recovered all six hundred yards of line. The sixty-pound leader had pulled free from the crimped sleeve, letting the fish get away with just a hook in his mouth.

Marlin have been known to sound to deep water, turn sideways, and fight to the death. After a large marlin dies in deep water, it is almost impossible to lift that much weight against the thermoclines and currents without breaking the line. More line would not have helped me. My only hope would have been a bigger rod, larger line, and more drag.

I knew where I would be next Fathers Day.

Gordon fighting Marlin

Mexico Hunting

Two weeks before Christmas I was antsy.

I asked Dad, "Where are we going hunting this year?"

"Dr. Kelly has a special trip for us to Mexico."

"Mexico! Wow! That's boss. How did he swing that?"

"Dr. Kelly's partner is Dr. DeBakey, the famous heart surgeon. They have a patient from Mexico, Juan Rodriguez. They saved Juan's life with a heart transplant, so Juan told Dr. Kelly to come down to his ranch to hunt anytime. That's where we're headed."

"This is gonna be so groovy. How many of us are going this year?"

"The same five fathers and six sons that went last year to Laredo. We head out the day after Christmas and stay for four days."

"This is a great tradition Dad. I get to spend time with you and my other friends on the coolest hunting trips."

Two weeks before Christmas we began preparations. Dad packed cold weather clothes, cleaned weapons, and bought ammunition. December in Texas and Mexico was brutally cold, requiring outdoorsmen to wear longjohns and heavy boots. The day after Christmas we met at Dr. Kelly's house to pack two 1966 Volkswagen buses with a full contingent of dogs, boys, food, booze, guns, thousands

45

of rounds of ammo, spare gas cans, and other supplies necessary to survive an expedition to Mexico. Dad and Dr. Kelly took cooking very seriously, so we stopped for a major soiree at a grocery store to buy enough food for a small army. The grocery expedition was an adventure unto itself, with a gang of camouflaged teenagers sporting gun belts, running up and down the aisles throwing food into the baskets and terrorizing the store in general.

By noon we were on the road to the border town of Eagle Pass, with five adults, (fortunately, including two doctors) in one van, while I rode in the other van with John Kelly and Jerry Abbot, who had just received their driver's licenses, and two other boys. I was fourteen years old, with the other boys ranging from twelve to sixteen. Three hours later we pulled up to the wide Rio Grande River and got out of the cars to stretch our legs. A thrill of anticipation ran though us as we looked at mysterious Mexico across the deep, muddy river.

I asked Jerry, "Have you been here before?"

"Naw, but my older brother came down to boys town with his fraternity. You wouldn't believe the women and beer they went through." We were too young to participate in those escapades, but we laughed nervously like we knew all about it.

Dad asked Doc, "Is crossing the border a problem? I hear there's been difficulties with drug smugglers this year."

"Don't worry. That was down in Laredo, not up here in Eagle Pass. I got it all lined up. Just smile and hand out twenties."

On the other side of the river was the border town of Piedras Negras. The mayor, Jorge Martinez, was another one of Dr. Kelly's patients. He met us on the American side of the bridge, sporting a black hat, black cowboy boots, black shirt, black pressed jeans, and black mustache.

Jorge gave Dr. Kelly a friendly handshake, asking, "Como esta?"

"I am great Jorge. How are you feeling?"

"Muy bueno, now that you fix my heart. What can I do for you amigo?"

"We would like to come over and spend a few days hunting in Coahuila. Do we need licenses?"

"There are no licenses in Mexico. Our people are too poor to hunt here and do not have guns. Come with me, Doctor. I take care of you. Give twenty dollars to each guard. They are all my cousins, so there will be no trouble. Remember you can't bring game back into the states."

Dr. Kelly responded, "Yes we know. We will give plenty of birds to the villagers as Christmas presents."

"I trust you will, Doctor. You're a man with a good heart."

"I'll see you next month for your check-up Jorge."

"Feliz Navidad."

Back in our cars, we followed him across the bridge and waited in line at the checkpoint. Dad and Doctor Kelly handed out twenties like candy to customs officers as they waved us through the checkpoint. This tradition, called mordida (the bite), has always been part of Mexican culture. While it was not legal to bring guns or ammo into Mexico, a little mordida to the Federales assured there were no inspections of our vehicles.

We left the United States to start the adventure in earnest. We entered a primitive world of cactus, rock, mesquite brush, and Mexicans. We drove an hour southward on the only paved road through the brush country. Pavement gave way to a rough, two-lane dirt road for two more hours, then narrowed down to one-lane. As we twisted through the head-high brush and cactus, we came upon the first of many mud-hut villages, called pueblos, where very poor peasants lived like in old western movies. There was no electricity and only a few trucks in the pueblos. It was the first time I had seen smoke drift over villages from wood fires used to cook and heat homes in the winter. The cold weather kept people indoors, making the villages appear to be smoky, empty, still-life photographs.

When we entered one un-named village of twenty huts, a black police car was menacingly parked across the road. With serious faces and macho attitudes, two fat Federales policemen stepped out of the car and sauntered toward us. In the boys van, we watched with concern when Dad and Dr. Kelly got out of their van and casually walked up to the police. After talking to the policemen for a few minutes, bills changed hands, and the smiling Federales waved us through.

A mile out of town, the adults stopped to laugh about the police stop and make hot buttered rum on Coleman burners to augment weak heaters in the old Volkswagens.

Twenty miles later, the road ended at a gate covered with cow skulls and barbed wire where Juan Rodriguez waited for us. With nervous anticipation we jumped out of the vans to stretch our legs. We were finally here, wherever that was. Juan slid out of his truck, adjusted his old cowboy hat, kicked his dusty boots, and shuffled over in a bowlegged swagger to meet Dr. Kelly.

With a firm handshake and big smile, Juan said, "This is the great Dr. Kelly who saved my life. Anything you want at my ranch is yours. Except mi espousa."

I asked, "Do you have any daughters?"

"Si. But I cut off your balls and kill you if you touch them."

We laughed, but knew he was serious.

"Follow me amigos. Just a few more miles."

We continued down the road, wondering if we would get to the ranch house before dark. Juan's spread was five thousand acres of scrub and brush ranch land. As the sun set, we finally pulled up to a large ranch house overlooking the Rio Grande Del Rancho River. This was our headquarters for the next three days. Juan's wife came outside to greet us.

"Doctor, we will have a real Mexican dinner after you unpack."

Ranch hands helped us unload our gear at the bunkhouses. One bunkhouse had a fireplace, while the other did not. I knew there would be a discussion later about sleeping arrangements, but right now hunger was the only thing on our minds.

We went back to the main house where a feast awaited us. We had a wonderful meal of freshly barbequed beef and goat, large pots of frijoles and rice, flour tortillas fresh off the grill, and bowls of jalapenos, onions, and tomatoes. This Mexican food had local spices and ingredients with a milder flavor than the Tex-Mex we were used to back home.

After we ate our fill, John Kelly asked, "Are you ready to shoot some rabbits?"

"You betcha," I replied.

"They're everywhere after dark. Lets get our guns."

Dad yelled, "Wait! You boys remember the rule."

We replied in unison, "Shoot what you want, but eat what you shoot."

We raced back to the vans, loaded up rifles, ammo, spotlights, and two Mexican boys to go on an unbelievable escapade of night hunting. This was a first for us because hunting at night was not legal in the States. The vans had two swiveling, rooftop chairs mounted on luggage racks. There were gun racks in front of the chairs and walkie-talkies to communicate with the driver.

I said, "Lets shoot for the first chair ride."

I threw a coke can out in the car headlights. Rifles blazed at the can, making it dance down the road.

"Stop!" I yelled. "Jerry and John hit it first. They get on top."

In this wild ranch land, game was everywhere. We drove down dirt roads and across fields at breakneck speeds, using spotlights to search for jackrabbits or occasional deer. We had semiautomatic 22-caliber rifles and shotguns. When we spied a rabbit, we chased it across fields and rocks with guns a blazing from the top seats and out the side windows. Though it was cold in the dark night, we were having too much fun to worry about being chilly. On the rough roads at moderate speeds, our accuracy was poor; but that made it all the more fun as we shot wildly at rabbits while they zigzagged through fields and brush. When we would hit a rabbit, a Mexican boy jumped out of the van and fetched it for us. We rotated seats between the roof and interior as rabbits were killed. It wasn't long before the back of the van was full of rabbits.

I finally said, "I have as many as I want to clean. Lets call it a night." We headed back to camp where our Mexican boys taught us how to clean rabbits.

In the states, dove and quail were the primary game birds. Down here in Old Mexico we also shot rabbits, roadrunners, meadowlarks, redbirds, and any other birds we saw. At the end of the day all of the game went into a big pot of stew. We found that all birds pretty much tasted the same, especially when stewed with onions, gravy, and jalapenos.

After cleaning our rabbits, we returned to the bunkhouse with a fireplace, only to find our fathers had claimed all the beds.

I asked Dad, "Where do we sleep?"

"You boys get the bunkhouse out back."

"But there's no fireplace."

Laughing, he said, "Wear your longjohns."

Jerry, John, and I looked at each other miserably. We grabbed our sleeping bags and headed to the dark, cold bunkhouse. We didn't mind too much since the excitement of actually being in Mexico kept us up horsing around most of the night.

Early the next morning, us boys were up for target practice on the river. We honed our accuracy by shooting hundreds of rounds with our light 22s as fast as we could reload them.

After breakfast we loaded up the vans for a days hunt and put on jackets, cactus proof chaps, heavy boots and warm hats. We hunted from both vehicles. The lead van had two gunners on rooftop chairs. The remainder of the hunting party rode anxiously inside the vans, ready to burst out with guns blazing when game was spotted. The rooftop seats were the choice positions with the most shooting, so we rotated stations every half hour, about as long as we could stand the cold wind blowing across the top of the van.

Jerry said, "Lets flip for top seats." We took out coins and flipped for the order of riding up top.

"Jerry," I said, "you and I are up first. Get your gun and coat ready."

The drill was to proceed at slow speed down a narrow dirt road barely wide enough for the vehicles. When the spotters up top saw a dove they shot right away, not an easy task on top of the bouncing car. The sky was thick with white wing dove, giving us plenty of targets. After a few hours of practice, I got to where I consistently hit the birds from the moving van. When we shot a dove, the van skidded to a stop, doors flew open, and our Springer Spaniels and weimaraners raced out to fetch the bird.

After a while, we topped a rise in the road where I saw the day's first covey of bobwhite quail running at twenty yards down the road.

"Stop!" I yelled into the walkie-talkie. "Quail in front of us."

When the van slammed to a stop, guys and dogs bailed out and the chase was on. Jerry and I grabbed our guns, stepped to the front roof, dropped down on our butts, slid onto the spare tire mounted on the front bumper, jumped to the ground, and took off running.

Weimaraners were excellent pointers, so we let them lead the way. Springer Spaniels were flushing dogs, not pointers. Dad kept them heeled behind us while the weimaraners followed the birds off the road and went on point at a big cactus patch, their front foot raised and quivering tails straight up. We slowly fanned out and approached the cactus with shotguns raised. When I saw a multitude of birds gathered in the cactus, I readied for fast and furious shooting by putting a spare shell in my teeth for a fourth shot.

Dad whispered, "Ready?"

When we nodded, he kicked the cactus pile. Dozens of quail exploded with thunderous fury in all directions in the most startling, adrenalin filled instant imaginable. The Springers left their heeled position and chased after the rising birds. Quail flew head high, zigzagging through brush as shot guns blasted all around me. I instantly pointed to a bird flying straight away and dropped it with a quick shot. I swiveled to the right and shot at another quail, but he rose up as I peppered cactus underneath him. I pumped another round into my twenty-gauge and tumbled the elusive bird with my third shot.

For eight seconds there was total chaos as eleven guns shot at birds flying in all directions in and out of cactus. Dogs jumped into the air after the quail, narrowly avoiding being shot. I rapidly grabbed the shell from my mouth and inserted it into my shotgun as three more late risers caught us by surprise. One flew between Dad and me. I hesitated until it passed Dad, and then shot as the bird disappeared behind another cactus clump, leaving a trail of feathers floating in the air.

Dad looked at me and said, "Good job waiting for a clear shot."

We reloaded and ran through the brush at breakneck speed following wounded quail. We chased stragglers for five more minutes before circling back to the van to regroup. The count was eleven quail. Not a bad way to start the day. We loaded up and headed down the road for more action.

Running through cactus and mesquite made it imperative to wear chaps and snake boots. By the end of the day, our poor dogs feet and legs looked like pin cushions full of cactus thorns. That night we spent hours with tweezers pulling cactus out of the moaning dogs. The next day we put boots on the dogs to reduce their misery. The boots offered cactus protection, but the dogs sure looked funny hopping around in red shoes.

When we rounded the next bend, I yelled into the walkie-talkie, "Blue tops on the right!"

Blue top quail were bigger than bobwhites. They were the marathon runners of quail, darting through the brush and refusing to fly until we ran right up on top of them. They would not hold tight and flush like bobwhites, they just kept running in small groups from brush pile to cactus patch. When chasing blues, we let the Springers charge out front, hoping to force the speedy birds to fly for an easy shot. Running after blues at full speed with shotguns off safety was a madhouse chase through the brush. I shot at quail on the ground, trying not to hit the dogs nipping at their tails. If I got close enough to the birds, one or two would flush, fly a few yards and then go back down. The blue tops scurried faster than we could run, so it became an endurance contest to see if we could flush them before we wore out. Of course, the boys chased the quail a lot further than the fathers.

At one point, Dad followed a covey of quail through the brush and tripped over a log. He dropped his shotgun and sprawled to the ground.

Through the brush I heard, "Oh no."

I pushed through the cactus to see Dad frozen flat on his stomach. His face was white as he stared at a rattlesnake as thick as his arm coiled up four feet away, rattling, and ready to strike. I instantly stopped. I didn't have a clear shot through the brush, so I waited to see what Dad would do. He stared the snake down and very slowly crawled backwards.

When Dad was out of striking range, I asked, "Want me to shoot it?"

"No, I want that son of a bitch." He retrieved his shotgun and made short work of the snake. He proudly marched back to the van with the six-foot snake raised head high.

I said, "Dad. You know the rules. You have to clean and cook that snake."

"Bring me a beer first," he replied. "I need to settle my nerves." That night the Mexican cook fried up fresh rattlesnake; and yes, it tasted like chicken.

Even more fun was the abundance of roadrunners, which were twice the size of quail. They really do run crazy like the cartoons, darting along the road or fence line rather than flying. One quick shot was all I would get before they disappeared into the brush. Chasing them in the van and shooting out the windows was the best bet because a roadrunner ran faster than a man.

When we stopped for lunch, a buzzard circled down and landed in a tree fifty yards away.

John smiled and asked me, "Think you can hit it?"

"Just watch." I leveled my 22 on the hood of the car and fired off a shot that knocked the buzzard out of the tree. We ran through the brush whooping and laughing, but pulled up short when we came up on one pissed-off bird.

It jumped all around, squawking with a broken wing while Jerry laughed at me, "Kill it, Gordon. Kill it."

I raised my shotgun and fired from ten yards. The impact knocked that tough buzzard down, but its heavy feathers stopped the birdshot from penetrating into the body. He jumped up and screeched again. I shot two more times with the shotgun, to no avail. That tough buzzard just kept getting up! We were flabbergasted.

Jerry finally said, "Use the 22." A couple of rounds finally put him out of his misery.

Dad came through the brush, "What is all this shooting about?"

Jerry and John laughed, "Gordon shot a buzzard. Does he have to eat it?"

With a big grin Dad said, "You know the rule, you shoot it, you have to eat it." I grimaced as the other boys roared with laughter.

After a day full of shooting, we returned to the ranch house where us boys cleaned a garbage can full of birds while the fathers drank beer and supervised. I got the cleaning drill down to where I could breast and skin a bird in seven seconds flat.

Then I had to clean that nasty, stinking buzzard. It took me thirty minutes of plucking feathers while my buddies roared with laughter, giving me a hard time.

We had a huge feast of stewed and fried game that night. The buzzard did not go into the main pot; rather, Juan cooked it separately just for me. I can honestly say that it did taste like chicken, only tougher. That was the last time I shot a buzzard, or any other animal of questionable taste.

After dinner we were resting in chairs, tired from chasing quail and dove all day.

John Kelly challenged us, "Ready to go night hunting again guys?"

I hesitated briefly, then replied, "Yeah, I'll go again."

I couldn't resist another round of chasing rabbits with spotlights. We had another crazy night of driving through the brush until we stuck the van in a ditch, miles from the ranch house. We dug, pried, and lifted for an hour until we pulled the van rose out of the ditch. That put a damper on chasing through the brush in the dark.

Jerry asked, "Wanna try something different?"

"Yes."

"I brought a dying rabbit call. Let's see if we can bring in a coyote."

John replied, "Cool. I never shot one of those."

We parked the van behind a brush pile and turned off the lights. Jerry and John went up to the top seats with a spot light and rifles. The rest of us settled onto logs in the brush, excited to try something new. The still moonless night was pitch black. There were no other lights for hundreds of miles. In the clean, cold air of the high Mexican plain, God's innumerous stars shined magically bright.

Jerry pumped the rubber call that squealed like an injured rabbit. Sightings of several coyotes during the day gave us hopes one would respond tonight. He waited two minutes and squealed again. Far away we heard the faint howl of a lonely coyote. We perked up, hoping Jerry could bring him into rifle range. Every five minutes he worked the call, loud and long, then soft and quick. After thirty minutes, the exercise of the day and stillness of the night caught up with me and I started drifting.

A sudden, high-pitched animal scream fifty yards in front of us shook me from my daze. *What the hell was that?* No one uttered a sound. I heard safeties clicking on guns. Thirty seconds later another ungodly shriek echoed fifty yards behind us. I crawled back to the van where the other guys were huddled up. Despite the dark of the night I saw the white of wide-open eyes.

I trembled with a death grip on my rifle, "What is that?"

Jerry whispered, "Mountain lion. He's got us surrounded."

Another terrible yowl fifty yards to the right melted us. Four of us on the ground scrambled to the top of the van, bending the chair frame and roof. We panted with palpable fear. Jerry shined the spotlight into the brush on our right, searching for the source of the terrible shrieks. The next scream was on our left! Guns shot blindly into the dark.

I yelled, "Lets get out of here."

We bailed off the roof, flung open the doors, and scrambled inside. Jerry started the motor, shifted into first, popped the clutch, and killed the engine.

"Hurry up," shouted John.

Jerry restarted the van, spun in a circle, and bounced wildly down the dirt road. In silence, we drove straight back to the ranch house, wondering what kind of cat had been stalking us.

The cold north wind made the bunkhouse miserably frigid. We built a huge bonfire outside, partly to stay warm and partly to keep creatures away. I put on extra heavy long underwear, laid down by the fire to get warm, then stumbled back to my sleeping bag in the bunkhouse. I couldn't wait until I was old enough sleep in the big house.

A few hours later I woke up shivering and mumbled, "God, I feel like an Eskimo." I stumbled out to the fire, fed it logs until I was warm, and then went back to my sleeping bag again.

John and I woke early the next morning to sneak down to the river where I had seen Canadian Geese the previous day. Sure enough, they were back in the same little cove on a sand bar. We crawled through the brush until we were very close, which surprised me because geese were normally very spooky.

I hissed, "Lets take 'em."

We jumped up and shot all four geese while they were still on the ground.

John asked, "Are they always that easy."

"I don't know? I never shot a goose before." We staggered back to camp carrying the heavy birds.

When we rounded the corner of the house, the cook ran out screaming, "El rancho gooso! El rancho gooso!"

How were we to know they were her pet geese? The rest of the gang rolled with laughter while the housekeeper screamed at us in Spanish. We didn't speak Spanish, but we sure got the gist of what she was saying. She calmed down after Dad gave her a few dollars.

At breakfast, the fathers discussed the day's plans.

Dr. Kelly asked Jaun, "Where do you think we should go today?"

"There's big deer up in Sierra Santa Rosa Mountains. It's a long ride, but you like hunting there."

Dad asked, "How far is it?"

"Maybe fifty miles. I take you."

"What do you think Doc? Can we make it that far today?"

"If we take extra gas and food I think we can get in some good hunting and maybe bag a big whitetail."

Dad replied, "Sounds good to me, Doc. Boys, lets get loaded up."

We pushed deeper into old Mexico, dads in one van drinking hot buttered rum, boys in the other. We gradually moved deeper south into high country, shooting a few birds along the way. Cactus and brush gave way to cedar trees and rock as we drove higher into the foothills. Our heavily loaded vans strained up steep roads, bouncing off rocks on the rough ride.

I asked John, "How far do you think we can get without four wheel drive?"

"With all you guys here to push, I'm not worried. As a matter of fact, the other van just got stuck. Too much rum. Out we go."

We pushed the dad's van off a rock for the third time.

I asked, "Juan, how much farther?"

He pointed. "Up to the next ridge."

Three hours out from the ranch, we finally came to the end of the road at an Indian village on the side of a mountain. The Indians had never seen white men before, so the villagers surrounded our vans, curiously looking at us and our strange vehicles. Dr. Kelly attempted to communicate them, but they did not speak Spanish. Luckily, Juan spoke their language. The village consisted of a dozen one-room log huts with no doors, windows, water, electricity, or bathrooms. Inside were dirt floors and a bucket for a toilet. Children played with a bear chained to the front door of one hut. This was dirtier and more primitive than any barnyard I had seen.

When the sun dropped early behind the mountains, we struck camp near the village and traded the Indians dove for fresh tortillas. Dr. Kelly put a pot of fresh chili over a bonfire and we feasted around the campfire telling stories. Hot buttered rum kept the dads warm, while the boys horsed around and snuck samples when the dads weren't watching.

I asked Jerry, "Have you camped in the mountains before?"

"No, this is my first time."

"Me too." I looked up at stars right on the mountaintops, twinkling like Christmas lights.

"Have you ever seen so many stars?"

"We're surrounded. I didn't know you could get so close to heaven. If my arm was just a little longer I know could reach up and grab one."

We huddled around the campfire to stay warm and watched the wondrous stars through clear mountain air. We put down sleeping bags, fed the fire, and fell asleep in the midst of stars twinkling around our camp.

The next morning, Indians told Juan we should follow animal trails up the mountain to find game. We walked up the rocky mountain on foot in single file. When the mountain became steeper, our pace slowed. Mark was walking in front of Harry. Harry slipped on a rock and came down on his shotgun. He had committed the cardinal sin of having the safety off. Boom! The gun went off and shredded Mark's new boot. Mark fell to the ground screaming in pain. In shock, we gathered round him as he writhed in misery.

Dr. Kelly looked at the bloody wound and said, "That should have taken his foot off. Good thing he had new boots on. I can stop the bleeding, but we need to get back to camp now! Fletcher, help me with a tourniquet."

Harry was white as a ghost. "I didn't mean to shoot him. What are we going to do?" This was not a pretty situation.

Dad said, "Everybody unload your guns now. Boys, we have to carry Mark down. Ya'll pick him up, but not by the foot."

Jerry anguished, "That could have been me."

John moaned, "Or me." The fun and games were over. We started the long climb back down the mountain with Mark twisting in agony. Back at the van, Dr. Kelly and Dr. Fletcher field cleaned the wound and shot Mark full of morphine. We bounced down the mountain road at breakneck speed in the vans for three long, miserable hours while Mark cried in agony with every bump. We made several stops for Dr. Kelly to change the dressing and give Mark more morphine. We were on our own, far from civilization.

We pulled up to the ranch house long after dark and immediately took Mark inside. The doctors cleared the kitchen table to create a makeshift operating room. They spent hours meticulously cutting dozens of BBs out of Mark's foot. While the heavy leather boots stopped most of the shot, the doctors could not reach numerous pellets deep in the heel bone. They worked on Mark much of the night, while the rest of us worried about Mark and silently packed for a long trip home. At sunrise, the somber group headed back to the States with little conversation.

We were not allowed by American Immigration to bring game back over the border, but the guns were okay. We stopped at villages along the way and gave away our game to hungry peasants. We crossed over the border and took the highway to San Antonio. The heavily loaded vans maxed out at fifty mph, making for another three hours of quiet introspection. We drove straight to a hospital, where surgeons operated for two hours to remove a dozen more pellets from Mark's heel bone. Because of the prompt care from Doctors Kelly and Fletcher, Mark eventually recovered with no permanent damage.

At the time we did not realize this would be the last of our Mexico expeditions. Border conditions rapidly deteriorated when drug smuggling picked up, making it impossible to take weapons across the border again. From then on we had father-son hunts in south Texas and told stories of wild Mexico.

Hole in the Wall

"Kevin, the tuna are running hard. You need to come over to Nassau this weekend."

The phone connection was bad from Nassau to Florida. I faintly heard his reply through the static, "Count me in. I'll book a flight for Friday. Whose boat are we going on?"

I yelled back, "Doctor Neil invited us to go on his twenty-six foot World Cat. You're gonna love it."

Kevin and I went to Dr. Greg Neal's house at sunrise Saturday, ready for a big day of deep water trolling. Doc was excited because he had heard reports of tuna caught only seven to eight miles north of Nassau. I had also been getting reports of fantastic catches of tuna at Hole in the Wall further north in the Abacos. I knew we were in for a great day fishing somewhere.

When we pulled out of the Nassau harbor, the wind was out of the southeast at ten knots, meaning our original plan to run forty miles southeast to the Exumas would be against a punishing wind. Doc decided to head north and use New Providence Island to shelter us from the wind. We trolled northward through the dark blue Caribbean Sea until noon, with nary a strike. By then we were twelve miles offshore with winds building to fifteen knots.

Doc said, "Fish gone. Wanna make a move to Hole in the Wall?"

Kevin looked at me. "Why not? Let's go for it."

We pulled in our lines and headed north for the thirty-eight-mile journey. Running with the wind, Doc pushed the throttles up to twenty knots. The catamaran's dual hulls sliced smoothly through moderate waves. An hour later we approached thirty-mile wide Northeast Providence Channel between Eluthera and Abaco. At that point, the Atlantic makes a big swing westward, past Grand Bahama, and on to the Gulf Stream off Florida. The westerly current mixed with southeasterly winds created angry three to four foot chopped waves that only hardy sailors ventured through. Half way across the channel, the ragged, isolated Hole in the Wall cliffs at the southern tip of Abaco appeared above the angry sea, guarded by a lighthouse atop tall cliffs. Out of the corner of my eye I saw a big splash in the water at fifty yards.

I pointed. "Look over there." A monster fish jumped completely out of the water, falling back with a splash.

Kevin said, "It must be a porpoise." The fish jumped repeatedly, high into the air and crashing down.

"That's as big as a porpoise, but its no porpoise," I exclaimed. "Its definitely a fish, but not a shark either."

Doc said, "That's a tuna." The fish jumped rapidly three more times.

Kevin replied, "That's bigger than any yellowfin I ever saw. Its three or four hundred pounds."

In awe, I said, "Boys, that's a bluefin tuna. They used to be all over the islands. Now there are just a few. Doc, you wanna try to catch him?"

"No way. We don't have reels that big. He would just mash our gear. Let's keep going to Hole in the Wall."

A few miles later we came upon a huge, yellow weed line stretching one hundred feet wide as far as we could see. We trolled for dolphin along one side of the weed line with Islander skirted ballyhoo. In short order, Kevin brought in a fifteen-pound dolphin. After we dropped baits out again, an even larger dolphin hit and Doc took his turn at fighting. The dolphin, looking every bit of 30 pounds, tail-walked across the ocean in an attempt to throw the lure.

I yelled, "Hang on Doc. Keep reeling. Don't let him get away."

Ten minutes into a hard fight on the bouncing boat, the dolphin was almost in range of the gaff. It jumped high again thrashing in anger and crashed into the water. The hook broke loose and flew back into the boat, almost hitting Doc. We were crushed with disappointment that such a fine fish had eluded us.

While dolphin were fun to catch, our target for the day was tuna. We pulled in our lines and kept moving northward toward Hole in the Wall, one of the best spots in the Bahamas for large tuna, dolphin, and marlin. A few hundred feet from the primordial cliffs, the water depth dropped almost straight down 6,000 feet along an underwater wall. Two miles offshore an underwater ridge rose to six hundred feet below the surface, causing an upwelling where baitfish and predators congregated. That was our secret destination.

We dropped large ballyhoo behind the boat and trolled across the ridge. At the peak of the ridge, one of the baits was slammed, making the Penn International 50 reel scream and bend the rod over. I grabbed the rod while Doc put a fighting belt around my waist. The initial run took two hundred yards of line out in seconds.

Kevin exclaimed, "Its gotta be a wahoo!"

I held on until the run was over, then tightened the drag and started the fight. I slowly pumped and reeled a few inches of line at a time. The rod tip jerked up and down in the stubborn wahoo headshake pattern. Twenty minutes later I had the fish next to the boat. Kevin expertly gaffed the twenty-eight-pound wahoo and swung it into the fish box. We slammed the lid as the wildly thrashing fish pounded so violently that the fiberglass fish box tore loose from its floor mounts and fell down onto the gas tank. We put cushions between the box and gas tank and kept going.

After an hour with no more fish biting, I told Doc, "Its four o'clock and we have a fifty-one mile run against the wind. We better head back home. We'll come back next weekend for more."

Reluctantly, he turned south toward Nassau and told me, "You take the first shift. Kevin and I will take a break."

I took the wheel while Doc and Kevin went into the cabin and attempted to sleep. With the rough seas, not much sleep was happening. Since we could only make seven or eight knots against the wind, I dropped a couple of marlin lures behind the boat. You never knew what lurked in these deep waters. If you didn't have a hook in the water you were guaranteed not to catch a fish. An hour and a half later, we were back on the original weed line halfway across the Northeast Providence Channel. When our lures passed through the weeds, a rod bent and shook again.

I yelled, "Fish on!" waking the guys up.

Kevin scrambled back to the pitching stern, wrestled the rod out of the holder, and brought a twenty-five-pound barracuda to the boat.

Doc teased, "Kevin, why you catching de barry?"

They went back to sleep while I kept navigated southeast straight into the wind-blown sea for two more hours until we passed out of the channel into calmer water near Harbour Island on the north end of Eluthera. A half mile away I saw a huge flock of brown noddy sea birds, locally called tuna birds, swirling in a frenzy, diving on small pieces of meat left by tuna tearing through baitfish.

I yelled, "Wake up guys. We got fish. There's also a frigate bird up high. Might be a marlin around here."

Kevin and Doc scrambled out of the cabin again and hurriedly changed baits to small, high-speed cedar plugs and plastic squid with eighty-pound fluorocarbon leaders. The fast moving tuna were hard to catch up with. I sped up to fifteen knots, pounding through the waves. Beneath the birds we saw a horde of tuna racing after baitfish. Inching in front of the school, I swung the lures in a large circle to intercept the fish, then slowed down. Two rods went down simultaneously and line blistered off the reels. Doc and Kevin grabbed the rods, pumping and reeling while I steered to keep the fish behind the boat. In no time, we had two hard fighting, fifteen-pound yellowfin tuna in the boat.

The birds and fish had moved a mile away while we were fighting the tuna. Five more adrenaline filled minutes of pounding through rough seas brought us to the birds again. When I pulled ahead of the school, Kevin and Doc dropped the lines back. Wham, three rods went down for a triple hook up. Chaos erupted on deck! Tuna crisscrossed each other in long powerful runs, entangling our lines and rods. We passed the rods around each other in a wild dance to keep the lines straight. I steered the boat and adjusted the throttle with one hand, holding my rod with the other hand. When I let go of the wheel to wind the reel, a wave caught us sideways and threw us around the boat like drunks as we laughed and cursed. Doc brought his fish in first. I put my rod in a holder and picked up the gaff as his fish approached the boat. When I bent down to gaff the tuna, I saw a seven-foot long shadow below the tuna.

I yelled, "Look at that marlin."

I quickly brought his skipjack tuna in and picked up my rod again. My fish fought hard for another five minutes. When it was thirty feet from the boat, the rod slammed down, the lure pulled free, and the line went limp. The marlin had taken my fish!

Meanwhile, Kevin was still fighting his tuna. All of a sudden his rod went down hard and the line screamed out. The marlin was running fast with his tuna. The billfish was lit up in neon blue and white when it sky rocketed out of the water and tail walked above the waves for twenty yards, shaking its head furiously. When it fell back to the water, the short, light leader used for tuna was instantly snapped. Intimidated by the power of the big fish, we stared in silence and realized we needed much heavier reels and lines to catch a mighty marlin.

The sun was now setting and we still had a long run ahead of us. The GPS showed Spanish Wells was ten miles to the east in Eluthera.

I told Doc, "Lets head over toward Spanish Wells until we get into cell phone range where we call the wives. They'll be getting worried."

The rough sea and fading sky kept our speed down as we passed the island. I was not looking forward to a night run. I never knew what logs, ropes, reefs, or other boats awaited us in the darkness.

I said to Doc, "We could get a hotel over there and drive back in the morning." He replied, "Naw, let's push on tonight."

"Its *your* boat, *you* have to drive in the dark in these treacherous reefs. I am not going to get blamed for wrecking your boat."

There was no way to see underwater reefs in the dark, but we could see the florescent white breakers warning us away. Kevin wasn't too excited about the reefs in the dark. He retreated to the cabin for the remainder of the trip while Doc and I stayed at the helm. When we picked up cell phone coverage three miles from Spanish Wells, Doc called his wife to notify her where we were, that we would be very late, and to call my wife.

Rather than take a straight, southerly course back across the open sea and rough water, we took a seventy-one mile curved route hugging the reef line for wind protection and better speed. We ran blind for three tortuous hours through a moonless night. We smashed through waves, following the GPS track through a maze of reefs past Atoll Island, Rose Island, Paradise Island, and Nassau. I stayed wide-awake, straining to see through darkness ahead of us. By now I was exhausted, running on overdrive from the long day; but there was no way I could go below and sleep.

When we reached the south side of Nassau to approach a narrow, unmarked channel to Doc's house, the GPS lost our track. The tide was low. We were blind and tired. We very slowly approached the shallow channel. Crunch. The boat jolted to a stop. Rats. The bow was firmly aground on a hard reef. I looked at Doc. One of us had to go overboard. I didn't want to tear up his props on the rocks, so I put my water shoes on and slipped over the side into black, knee-deep water. I tried not to think about sharks, barracuda, or razor sharp coral. Ten feet behind the boat, waves rippled marking the edge of the deeper channel. Doc raised the engines and reversed them when I pushed on the bow. No good. The boat was too heavy. I waited for a small wave to gently raise the boat a few inches, then gave a big heave. The boat ground six inches backward. I went into a pattern. Wait for another wave. Lift again, gaining a few more inches. When I took my next step forward, my foot went into a hole of sharp coral that cut my shin. Damn blood. Sharks hunt at night. I kept pushing. I gained a few more feet, finally breaking the boat loose into deeper water. That's when a gust of wind grabbed the stern and swung it around. Crunch again. This time the boat was crossways to the wind with the whole bottom grinding on the coral with each passing wave.

Doc asked, "Hey buddy. You okay?"

"Yeah, gotta start over. I'm sure am glad it's not my boat." I slowly waded back to the stern in a fog, gingerly checking with each step to avoid holes in the reef. With the next rising wave I walked the stern out to the edge of the channel.

"Doc, it is deeper back here. Drop the engines a little and see if you can pull us off this damn reef."

The propellers grabbed enough water to keep the wind from swinging the boat around again. Back to the bow I walked. Tired. Back hurts. Start the cycle again. Push, step. Push, step. Inch by inch we worked the boat back to the channel, finally pulling free. I grabbed the rail when Doc gunned the engine, struggling to pull myself into the boat. I fell onto the deck in exhaustion.

At long last, we pulled into Doc's dock at eleven thirty, relieved to be back on solid land. After two more hours of cleaning the boat and fish, Kevin and I made the thirty-minute ride home, completely zoned out. I was glad there was no traffic on the read. By the time we refrigerated the fish and cleaned up, it was three o'clock. Kevin and I called it a day and hit the sack exhausted, dreaming of the marlin that got away in the wild sea of Abaco.

Greg, Christopher, and Courteney Neil and Gordon
with fish from Hole in the Wall

Boat Tales

Rabbit Run

Gordon shifted his Hodaka Super Rat 100 cc motocross bike into third gear, wrapped the throttle wide open, and flew off the bank of the creek right behind his best friend, Steve Craig, on an identical Super Rat. Gordon knew Steve cautiously slowed down on the jumps. Gordon planned to pass Steve by aggressively charging through the jumps and whoop-de-doos. He thought, *I gotcha now*, as the engine maxed out at 10,000 rpms. He sailed over Steve's head at thirty miles per hour. Fifteen feet later he landed in the bottom of the dry creek, a few scant feet ahead of Steve on the narrow dirt track. When the wildly spinning knobby back wheel hit the ground and bit in, the front wheel tried to violently lift up and flip Gordon onto his back. He leaned over the handlebars and held the front wheel to a two-foot high rise in a high-speed wheelie. Gordon leaned left to cut Steve off and take command of the rut in the bottom of the creek. A split second later, they crossed the wide creek bed and flew up the opposite bank. Gordon shifted into fourth gear and accelerated up the hill. After he hit the top of the bank, he continued rising to five feet of air, extending his lead over Steve. Now he was just behind Billie's 125 cc Hodaka Combat Wombat. With a lightening fast shift into fifth gear at full throttle without the clutch, Gordon's Super Rat jumped closer to the Wombat as they entered into a long, sweeping curve in the dirt course. All three bikes screamed insanely loud through

73

modified straight pipes with only token mufflers, thereby increasing speed and sound to the max. Only the helmets kept the sound of the bikes to a bearable level.

They were in north Dallas on the Rabbit Run motocross course full of creeks, woods, and trails. They were practicing for a big Fourth of July race in Garland with a fifty dollar first prize, big bucks for eighteen year olds in 1972. The reckless, invincible racers had been at it neck and neck for the last hour. The hot July sun drenched them with sweat and the dry dusty track blackened their teeth.

Billie kept a small lead on his stronger bike through an empty straightaway. Gordon was right on his tail, with Steve just inches to the rear. Gordon was at full throttle in fifth gear at fifty miles per hour when Billie slowed for a curve to the left. Gordon inched passed Billie, jumped up and came down hard on the foot brake, leaning to the left to cut Billie off and maintain power through the long sweeping curve.

That's when the brake cable broke.

Gordon silently screamed, knowing he would not make the turn. He was in a high-speed full-power slide trying to turn left. However, without his brake, he slid straight ahead toward a blur of green trees on the right side of the curve. If he backed off the throttle he would lose control of the slide and flip over into a deadly wreck.

Going into a slow motion death sequence, he flashed, *HEERREE COOMMESS the FIIRRSTT RROWW of TRREESS*. Whack, whack, whack. The sideways bike slowing down to thirty mph as it mowed down small saplings.

74

The big trees came up fast. He aimed straight ahead and downshifted to get back on the power curve. This blur of events happened in a flash.

All Steve and Billie knew was that Gordon had passed them, but when he threw the bike into a slide he didn't slow down; he went straight ahead into the woods. They quickly stopped their bikes and ran back to the edge of the woods where they followed a path of torn up brush and dirt through a cluster of two-foot diameter oak trees. Breaking through the oaks, they couldn't see Gordon; but the scream of his engine told them they were near. Ten more yards and the trail of broken trees and brush disappeared into the bottom of a creek. Gordon had fallen off the creek bank into shallow water with the bike on top of him. The motor still screamed at full throttle. He lay there dazed until Steve ran up, turned off the engine, and pulled the bike off of him.

Steve asked incredulously, "Are you okay?"

Gordon shook his head to clear the cobwebs and muttered, "I think so. Damn brake cable broke. I didn't think I was going to make it through all those trees."

Billie chided, "You picked a heck of a way to cool off."

Billie and Steve drug the bike out of the creek and walked it back through the newly created path through the trees while Gordon staggered behind them. They stopped when the three-foot wide handlebars wouldn't pass through a narrow gap between two large oak trees. Steve looked back at Gordon incredulously.

"How did you get your bike through these trees?"

Gordon paused to reconstruct the blur of the last few minutes.

"Piece of cake. When I saw the big trees coming at me I straightened out of the slide to face forward. Right before I hit the trees, I aimed at a gap, popped a wheelie, and turned the handlebars ninety degrees to clear the trees with just inches to spare on each side. After I got through the trees, I brought the wheelie down, but still had no brakes. The saplings slapped my handlebars until I slowed down. Like to broke my hands. Then I fell into the creek. I can't believe I made it, I should have hit a tree and killed myself."

"You got that right," said Steve. "That was incredible riding."

"How does my bike look?"

"Other than no brakes, the handle bars are bent a little. You'll be able to drive home. Gordon, you're one lucky son of a bitch."

"I know, I just used another one of my nine lives. Let's go home, boys. I've had all the fun I can stand for one day. We'll come back tomorrow and practice again. I have a brake cable to fix."

Steve laughed, "I'll beat you tomorrow."

Sailfish at Pinas Bay

Big Dolphin

While living in Nassau, my fishing buddies had the coconut telegraph set up to ring when the fish were biting. I heard a March dolphin run was in full swing in the Exuma Islands, so Kristian Kwiecinski, Gary Honkofsky, and I loaded up *Boat Tales* to partake of the fun. We were a good team, well experienced with dolphin frenzies. Each spring swarms of dolphin, mahi-mahi, migrated through the Bahamas following bait schools northward, eventually ending up near Cape Hatteras in the summer.

We made a fast forty-mile run across smooth flats from Nassau to Ship Channel Cay at the northern end of the Exumas, a string of rocky, barren islands with turquoise flats on the west and indigo water of Exuma Sound on the east.

At low tide, we passed through a narrow cut between small, nameless islands. Perched on the bow, Kristian guided us through a maze of treacherous four-foot waves breaking over shallow reefs. One-half mile later, we went from watching the rocky bottom in fifty feet of crystal clear water, to the abrupt 2,000-foot drop of the reef wall into a blue abyss.

We lowered ballyhoo baits into deep water and trolled northward along the edge of the wall towards the "pocket," where the islands swung through a curve from north to east. Southeast winds trapped extraordinary numbers of baitfish along the reef wall where predator fish awaited. The resulting feeding frenzy created the best location in the Bahamas to catch dolphin during their spring run.

We set short teasers in the motor's wake, and then dropped naked ballyhoo baits behind those. We used ballyhoo with pink or green skirts on high outrigger poles that spread two more lines one hundred feet behind the boat. A shotgun rod with a blue and white islander lure was deployed from the second story rocket launcher. Its bait was set one hundred yards back to attract cautious predators stalking the boat.

In short order we landed a double header of twenty and twenty-two pound dolphin from the outriggers. I deposited the fish into a six-foot long fish bag tied against the inside wall of the cockpit. The bag was custom made with the same insulation used on a space shuttle. A bag of ice would keep 100 pounds of fish cold all day long. After re-baiting, I resumed trolling for more action.

Shortly after that, we heard the thrilling buzz of the clicker on the big Penn International 50 reel of the shotgun line.

I yelled, "Fish on," grabbed the rod off the tower, and passed it to Kristian. He reared up hard to set the hook into a fish far behind the boat. The rod tip jerked down almost to the water, a sure sign of a big fish. Gary pulled in the other lines to clear the deck for a fierce battle. A minute later the reel was still screaming. The addictive adrenaline rush of a primordial struggle kicked in. This high was why we worked so hard and spent so much money pursuing deep-water fish.

Gary shouted, "He's not slowing down, better start after him."

I carefully turned the boat and gunned the throttle to chase a four-foot dolphin greyhounding across the water 150 yards behind the boat. Kristian gained line as we raced in pursuit. When we neared the fish, it sensed the boat and dove deep. This fish was not about to surrender just yet. Kristian strained his arms and back to slowly lift the dolphin a few inches at a time. Fifteen minutes later, the angry green brute saw the boat and launched into another run, taking back hard won line. After another five minutes of struggle, Kristian brought the big bull dolphin up from the deep again. I kept the boat at a slow speed to keep pressure on the fish and to keep him from circling around the boat.

"I see color," Gary shouted. "He's at least a thirty pounder."

I told Kristian, "Keep it away from the prop or you'll lose it."

Gary yelled, "He's diving under the boat. Turn right."

I swung the boat around hard, and then replied, "Take the wheel. I'll do the gaffing." I unzipped the top of the fish bag in preparation for landing the large catch.

When Kristian pulled the fish close to the boat, I swung hard with the gaff and pulled the thrashing dolphin out of the water, swung it across the boat, and dropped it into the fish bag. Before I could pull the zipper closed, the angry fish rebounded out, slinging blood and slime all over the boat. When the flapping fiend landed between my legs, I tried to sit on it. The slippery fish slithered away, bounced across the boat between Kristian and Gary, landed on the gunwale, and splashed into the water before we could lift a finger! We were stunned, frozen in silence over the loss of a great fish.

I grimly told the guys, "We are *not* going to lose another fish." We silently re-rigged and dropped baits back into the water.

Ahead of us I saw several boats fighting fish, so I headed their direction, knowing we would soon be into dolphin again.

Gary bellowed, "Here she comes." He point fifty yards to the starboard where a brilliant gold cow dolphin bounded across the water. She charged our spread of lures, jumping into the air every two to three seconds.

I shouted to Gary, "Grab that outrigger rod and get ready." The three-foot cow flew into the air, back flipped with the bait in her mouth, and crashed into the water.

Kristian yelled, "Wow!"

Gary held tightly on to the bent rod while the fish took off on her first run. Ten minutes later I gaffed the twenty-six pound dolphin and threw her in the fish bag, closing it immediately before we had another escapee.

I said, "Let's get those lines back in the water, guys. The bite's really hot. We're gonna fill up the boat today."

"Yeah man," replied Kristian, grinning from ear to ear. "The next one's mine."

Gary responded, "Not if I grab the rod first."

We quickly rebaited and watched for more fish. Soon Kristian hooked into another twenty-five pounder, rapidly bringing it to the gaff. By now the fish bag was full.

I reminded the guys, "Don't worry, we have the spare fish box. Let's get some more of these bad boys."

When the action slowed for a while, we broke out lunch. A sure fire way to attract fish was to eat a sandwich, but I was still surprised when a huge bull dolphin flew out of the water right behind the boat and hit a bait behind hookless teasers near the engine.

Choking on my sandwich, I spun back to the wheel and yelled; "Fish on."

Gary grabbed the rod and was almost pulled into the water when he tightened the drag. The monster fish took off across the stern crossing two other lines.

I shouted, "Clear those lines."

Kristian and I frantically grabbed the other rods and passed them over and under Gary's rod, trying to untangle the mess. The fish had Gary pulled up tight against the back rail, making it difficult to maneuver the rods around him. We looked like the three stooges as we yelled, scrambled, and frantically reeled lines.

Gary pleaded, "Get me a belt! This rod is killing my stomach."

Kristian mocked, "Poor Gary, the fish is hurting his stomach." Kristian and I laughed while we struggled to strap a fighting belt on Gary as the fish tried to pull him overboard. We watched in amazement while the big bull made a two hundred yard run.

"Just hang on," I told Gary. "You can't stop the first run on a fish like this. He has to tire on his own."

When the fish finally slowed, Gary tightened the drag, pumped the rod, and started reeling. He lifted, dipped, and reeled while I chased the fish with the boat. If I rushed up on the dolphin while it was still green, it would dive under the boat and cut the line on the prop. I steered at slow speed to keep the fish off the stern, waiting for it to tire. The fish was huge. Gary struggled to gain line inch by inch. After twenty minutes, we saw color when the fish rose from the deep. I let go of the wheel and grabbed the gaff, knowing the hydraulic would keep *Boat Tales* moving in a straight line.

I shrieked, "Look at the size of that son of a bitch. That's the biggest dolphin I've ever seen! No screw-ups this time. Kristian, open the fish box and get ready. This one's not getting away."

Suddenly, the dolphin rocketed completely out of the water. The mad bull was eye-to-eye with me as he back flipped, angrily staring with defiance before he splashed back into the water and began another blistering run. Gary was slammed into the side of the boat again. This fight was far from over.

Kristian said, "Keep reeling. Get him back here before he spits the hook, unless you want Gordon to show you how to reel." Gary grunted and strained his arms while we laughed.

I told Kristian, "Grab the wheel and steer to the right. He's trying to circle."

The mammoth dolphin gave us an incredible aerial show, jumping and flipping across the water. Every time it jumped, I hoped it wouldn't cut the line with its tail. For every three feet of line Gary reeled in, the fish would take back four.

"Keep reeling," Kristian coached. "If you rest, he'll rest and take off again. If you don't hurry up, a shark will take him."

Gary moaned, "This damn fish is killing my arms."

I told him, "Keep reeling and pump with your legs, not your arms. Tighten the drag some more. We're still a long ways from getting this fish into the boat. We have to do everything perfect or we'll lose him."

82

Bringing in the big fish was a team effort, with Gary reeling, me at the gaff, and Kristian driving the boat to keep the fish positioned off the stern. When the dolphin tried to swim in front of us to circle the boat, Kristian sped up and turn the opposite direction. Then the shrewd fish dove back toward the prop. Kristian turned violently in the other direction, throwing us around the boat.

After ten more minutes of fierce battle, Gary had the fish back to the side of the boat. It was crucial to gaff it in the head for optimum leverage and control, swing the fish smoothly across the boat, and put it into the fish box recessed in the floor. I hoped my back was strong enough to lift this giant out of the water. I'd never lifted a fish this big. When I reached down with the gaff, the fish dodged and dove under the boat.

I screamed, "Keep clear of the prop. Steer to the right." When Gary reached over the side and put the rod tip into the water, he lost all leverage and almost fell overboard. I grabbed his belt and pulled him back from the thrashing fish. With the drag tightened all the way, the fish was also pulled up. He kept coming up and jumped completely out of the water again next to the motor, then splashed down, drenching us. We cursed and scrambled wildly. The mayhem was incredible.

I yelled, "Steer to the left." After five more minutes of fierce fighting on the rod, Gary had the fish next to the boat for the third time.

I told Kristian, "Slow down and let him come up where I can gaff him." The fish came closer. Closer. I made a vicious stab with the gaff in a sweeping motion and swung the thrashing dolphin over the rail hard and fast. God he was heavy. I couldn't get him across the boat and into the fish box, so I threw the struggling fish onto the floor of the boat and fell on him. Gary and Kristian also dove onto the beast, pinning it to the deck. The fish was really mad, bucking like a bull. The rod, gaff, line, hook, blood, and guts flew everywhere. We struggled, yelled, and cursed to keep the slippery dolphin in the boat. After several minutes of riding the bouncing beast, I managed to put a towel over his eyes to calm him down. I opened the fish box, slid him in, and slammed the lid closed, only to find the head and tail sticking out from each end of the five-foot box. The fish was a full six feet long!

I told Gary, "Sit on that lid until your fish is dead." After a few more thrashes, the fish was finally subdued. Covered with blood and slime, we whooped and hollered.

"We did it. Great job Gary!"

"Oh my aching arms, I can't move."

I pulled out a scale to weigh the monster. When I lifted him up, the scale bottomed out at fifty pounds.

I grinned. "We need a bigger scale." From the hold I retrieved a larger scale.

"I'm glad I finally get to use this big one." I lifted again.

"That's a fifty-five pounder, the biggest dolphin ever for *Boat Tales*. Way to go guys." We paused to admire the huge bull and catch our breath.

I thought about it for a moment and concluded, "I don't know about you guys, but I have had enough. We have more fish than we know what to do with. What do you say we call it a day?"

Sheer Terror

Little did I know how very close I would come to facing down death on that beautiful spring day. At the time I worked as a Civil Design Engineer in Nassau. I slowly drove into the seedy part of town, responding to a citizen complaint about a cave-in on a large ditch that ran along the backyard of a row of broken down crack houses. Driving up to the dilapidated house, I had no trepidation or premonitions about the neighborhood; I had learned to go anywhere in his government car without fear. It never occurred to me to be afraid today.

I stepped out of the car and approached the house. The smell of rotten garbage wrinkled my nose. It did not appear anyone was home; the unpainted front door was closed, stringy cloth shades were drawn over the windows, the crooked garage door was down, and there was no car in the driveway. The grass was unmowed, no fences between the houses, no trees in the yard. There was a broken down, rusted out car resting on blocks in the back yard, typical in this gloomy, desperate area.

Following standard procedures, I walked up to the broken porch and knocked on the front door to inform the homeowner that I was responding to a complaint. When no one answered, I thought, 'I'll just slip around the back yard and make a quick inspection to see what the problem is with the ditch.' When I nonchalantly strolled between the houses, I was more focused on the condition of the ditch than anything else.

Out of the corner of my eye I noticed that, unlike the front yard, there was very little grass in the backyard. That's strange, I thought. Suddenly, thundering footsteps coming from around the corner of the house thirty feet away made me spin to my right. Then I saw it. A huge, muscular, sixty pound, brown and white pit bull barreling down at me in full attack mode!

The dog had instinctively kept quiet when I approached, but now erupted in a crescendo of snarling and barking, fully intending to intimidate and kill me. And it worked!

I had grown up around dogs and learned that often the best response to an aggressive dog was to show no fear and face it down. That was not going to work this time. Not with this dog.

The sheer terror of impending attack and death came over me like a thunderbolt, and for the first time in my life I was truly afraid of dying. Knowing I was only seconds away from death, I went into the slow motion death sequence seen in movies. I desperately tried to spin around to make an impossible run for it. Total fear consumed me while the dog continued his seemingly unstoppable vicious charge.

There were no trees nearby to climb. My only hope was to make it to the old rusty car ten feet away and somehow climb on top of it before the dog struck. I took one long, agonizingly slow step toward the car and then another. I felt like I was running through a pool of oil with a ball and chain. When I realized I was not going to make it, I looked over my shoulder and prepared for the brutal attack. I didn't even have time to raise my arms in self-defense when the dog jumped – hit the end of his chain - and back flipped!

Oh My God! The dog bounced to his feet and lunged again. He flipped again, snapping and snarling. Unbelievably, the chain held fast!

I staggered away, adrenaline pouring through my veins, heart pounding, and gasping for breath. I was not dead. I had never known such sheer terror. I lurched to my car, crawled in, and sat there dazed. I felt like my chest would explode while I hid in the safety of the car. Would I survive the dog only to die from a heart attack?

A few deep breaths and five minutes later, I was just steady enough to drive white knuckled, back to the office.

When I walked inside, my buddy Greg said, "You're white as a ghost! What happened?"

I told my story and Greg and my coworkers howled with laughter. I, however, didn't see the humor and remained shaken. An hour later my adrenaline was still pumping and my heart still pounded.

I rose from my desk and told Greg, "I can't work anymore today."

I and headed home for a stiff drink, thinking that today's dance with death was just a little too close.

John Lyon, Bob England, Tommy Hill,
and Gordon with sheephead and jackfish
at Port Aransas

Pinas Bay

"Sailfish!" the captain yelled, pointing off the starboard bow where three billfish languished on the surface just forty feet from the boat. He made a turn to bring four strip baits and two daisy chain squid teasers in front of the sailfish. One responded by charging past the strip baits and into the daisy chain twenty feet behind the boat. The mate reeled in a strip-bait and positioned it just behind the teasers. When the blue and purple neon sailfish savagely attacked the strip bait, the mate dropped the line back for an eight count, then without pumping, reeled to pull the circle hook tight. Fish on!

The mate handed me the rod and my first Pacific sailfish was on an awesome run, tail-walking away from the boat for fifty yards. I climbed into the fighting chair and prepared for battle. Another hundred yards of thirty pound line was off the reel before the fish stopped. I pumped and wound for ten minutes, watching the angry billfish put on an aerial show on top of the water. When I the fish was close enough to see the boat, he took off on another run. The captain backed down on the sail for five more minutes before the mate grabbed the leader and pulled the one-hundred pound fish over the gunnel for pictures. I stared straight into the big, black, angry eye, kissed the head, and returned the exhausted fish back to the sea. The mate pulled the sail alongside the boat until it was revived, then released it. What a fantastic start to fishing in Pinas Bay, Panama.

Dr. Greg Neil from Nassau, his brother Sheldon Neil from Jamaica, and I were on an extraordinary fishing trip at the Tropic Star Lodge. I met Dr. Neil in Nassau, where I had lived for the last two years. We became great friends and fished together across the Bahamas on our boats. We had watched the ads for Tropic Star in the fishing magazines for several years, dreaming of this trip.

I finally told Greg, "Let's stop talking and go down to Panama next spring and see if the fishing is as good as they say."

"We'll make a move Gordon. Put it together."

The Tropic Star Lodge was routinely featured in fishing magazines, the Robb Report, and ESPN as the best saltwater fishing resort in the world. Famous fishing artist Guy Harvey adopted Tropic Star as his favorite place to fish and shot several shows about world-class bill fishing in Pinas Bay. His original paintings of full size fish adorned the walls of the Lodge, bringing smiles to fishing guests.

The Tropic Star Lodge boasted over 250 world records from their fleet of fifteen thirty-one-foot Bertrams. The number of fish caught in Pinas Bay was staggering. Their best bite was during one week in 2006, when over 1,200 sailfish were caught, while 77 marlin were caught and released in January 2007. Catching a grand slam of blue, black, and striped marlins was a common feat during winter marlin runs. As a matter of fact, the lodge guaranteed a marlin catch during August and September, or it would refund a customer's airfare. With these kinds of numbers, we knew we were in for a real treat.

The Tropic Star Travel Agency in Orlando handled bookings for the trip, providing experienced and friendly agents that took care of every detail with first class style. When we landed in Panama City on Copa Airlines direct from Orlando, we were met at the gate by Tropic Star agents and whisked through Customs to the VIP lounge. While we waited for our luggage to unload and clear customs, we sampled local food and Balboa beer. We learned that English is widely spoken in most areas of Panama. We were taken by van to the Bristol Hotel, one of the finest five-star, small hotels in the world. Rooms were priced at a very reasonable $120 per day. Service was impeccable, with butlers and maids at our beck and call. The hotel restaurant had gourmet cuisine with some of the best food anywhere, and priced less than twenty dollars a meal.

We arrived in Panama City three days early to explore the city before moving on to fishing. Contrary to my preconceived notions, Panama City was a vibrant, wealthy town with a skyline matching large U.S. cities. Over a dozen skyscrapers under construction attested to the strength of their economy funded by Panama Canal revenues. Casinos were abundant and all American fast food restaurants were present.

Due to our long military presence in Panama, U.S. construction standards were adopted for buildings, roads, streetlights, drainage, water, and sewer. The water was even drinkable through most of the City. In many areas of Panama City, Spanish signs were the only clue of being in another country.

The next day we toured the Mira Flores locks of the Panama Canal, one of the wonders of the world. There was a spectacular four-story museum and visitor center highlighting the canal's thirty-three year construction effort. We also toured six French and Spanish colonial sections of town that dated back to the 1400's.

On our third day, we boarded a small plane for an hour ride to Tropic Star airstrip on the Pacific coast near the Columbian border. The lodge was surrounded by over 1,400,000 acres of the Darien National Park, a UNESCO World Heritage Site, and Biosphere Reserve of Humankind. The nearest road was one hundred miles away. Mike and Terri Andrews, CEO/Operators from Orlando, managed the lodge. The topography was a stunning, mountainous, rain forest with hundreds of indigenous species of birds and animals.

The folks at Tropic Star were among the founders of CONAMAR Foundation that promoted conservation and protection of nature, the environment, and marine species in Central America. They were the first in the region to instigate the use of circle hooks in tandem with a catch and release program. They also promoted the government's ban on tournaments and commercial fishing that killed large numbers of billfish. When fishing from the lodge, only a few of the smaller species were kept each day to feed the guests, with the remaining fish released.

From the airstrip, a panga boat took us for a short ride down the Jaque River to the Tropic Star Lodge docks. Viewed from our water-side approach, lush forest hid most of the Lodge's facilities nestled on the side of a tropical mountain covered in a dense rainforest. At the bar we met fishing fanatics from all over the world who were drawn to these legendary waters to catch record-breaking fish.

Many had brought their own custom built rods and reels in their quest to break records.

The Lodge slept thirty-six guests in clean, well-kept bungalows. Rooms on top of the mountain were accessed by a tram ride up the steep slope through the jungle. Facilities included a beautiful pool, tiki bars, restaurants, and cabanas in rich tropical vegetation. Dinners were superb offerings of freshly caught seafood cooked by gourmet chefs.

On our first afternoon, we were taken on a panga ride for a quick run to throw lures along a rocky shore. In short order, Sheldon caught the first roosterfish of the trip before the afternoon rains drove us back to the tiki bar for rum drinks. Dinner that night was an outdoor Bar-B-Q of pork, ribs, and juicy fish covered with fresh mango salsa. Native dancers and musicians entertained us under tropical stars in the stunning jungle paradise.

The next morning, coffee was delivered to our door at five-thirty. After a quick breakfast, the fleet left at six-thirty, with the first order of business being to catch fresh bait. After a five-mile run from the Lodge, we came upon acres of baitfish swarming along the shoreline. We dropped two feather jigs into the sea and positioned them twenty feet back on small diameter cords tied to the cleats on each side of the boat. The cords had a heavy bungee cord spliced into their middle to absorb the shock of a strike. Two more feather jigs were dropped back fifty-feet on rod and reels.

Six boats from the Lodge circled the school of bait and quickly brought in bonita, skipjack tuna, hound fish, Pacific sierra mackerel, and other species on hand lines and rods. The abundance of baitfish was staggering, which explained the heavy presence of predator fish. Multiple hookups had lines crossing in chaos. We even had sailfish jumping among the bait, giving us a preview of action to come. After catching a day's supply of bait, the mate filleted belly strips from bonita and sewed them around circle hooks.

We dropped baits just a mile offshore and trolled two hours without a bite. At eleven-thirty, we received a call on the radio from another boat that fish were sighted. All six Tropic Star boats rushed in to see sailfish crashing a bait school. Within five minutes each boat had rods bent with sails tail-walking in pandemonium. The expert captains jockeyed boats to keep lines and fish from tangling each other. Over the next hour we caught and released five spectacular Pacific sailfish weighing over one hundred pounds.

When the bite stopped, we trolled along the shoreline backdropped by soft, high mountains. Rainy season had just begun, causing mountaintops to slip in and out of site as white, wispy clouds danced across the rain forest. Rugged mountains were eerily half hidden with rain that fell sporadically in patches across their sides. I sensed the strength of primordial mountain gods watching us somberly from above. The remoteness of raw nature reminded me of Marlin Brando at the end of the river jungle in *Apocalypse Now*. No telephones, computers, TV, cars, or radio; just the sound of boat engines and waves breaking on the rugged rock shore.

The bite soon started again and we brought three more sailfish to the boat. That is, Sheldon and I caught sails. Greg caught plenty of jacks, but no sails that day. At three o'clock sharp, lines were brought in and we returned to the Lodge where the dock master was very attentive to the incoming boats, recording each species of fish caught by each angler, number of hook ups, and size of fish. Tropic Star Lodge's philosophy of game management served as a sterling example for guides everywhere.

The next day, we fished the shoreline for snapper and roosterfish. After catching live bait, the captain slow-trolled close to a deep, rocky shoreline. Heavy rods with drags tightened up on 50-pound line were used to try to keep powerful reef fish from diving for the rocks to cut the lines.

Smash! A powerful fish hit a bait and headed for the rocks. This fish was STRONG, bending the rod violently and stripping line off the reel at an amazing rate. I had no doubt this fish was a member of the amberjack family, which was known for being bullies of the reef. Greg grabbed the rod and was pulled against the rail. It was all he could do to hold on against the tight drag. The Captain steered the boat to pull the brute away from the rocks. After ten minutes of gaining line inch by inch, we saw spectacular black and white stripes identifying the roosterfish. Before the rooster could be gaffed, it took off on another brutal run. Greg struggled with the reel again, while Sheldon and I yelled and laughed at him.

I said, "I told you to start working out last month and lifting weights. You didn't think you needed to work out. What do you think now?"

He just grunted as his arms and back cramped. After another five minutes of muscle against fish, Greg brought the roosterfish back to the boat. When it saw the boat again, it took off on a third run! This fish was incredibly strong. Greg moaned, but kept reeling while Sheldon and I looked on in awe and trepidation. We wondered if we really wanted to catch one of these stubborn fish ourselves.

Soon the mate grabbed the leader and brought in the thirty-pound roosterfish. The long, soft dorsal fins were beautiful reminders of our tropical habitat. Greg struggled to hold the thrashing fish for a quick picture and then returned it to the sea for the next angler.

The captain turned around and trolled by the same rocky point again. Slam went a rod. When I picked it up, I thought I had a runaway horse. I used all my strength in a vicious tug of war. I was determined to win. After a harsh twenty-minute battle, I had a forty pounder in the boat. This was incredibly fun! Roosterfish were harder fighting than a hundred-pound sailfish that jumped to exhaustion in just a few minutes.

We trolled the shoreline the rest of the day, ending up with a mixed bag of six roosterfish, along with many jacks and mackerel. We even caught a wildly jumping houndfish that looked like a giant needlefish. The captain estimated the weight at twenty pounds, but I thought it weighed more. The mate was excited and immediately filleted the delectable, white meat for dinner. The teeth and bones of this strange tropical fish were a brilliant, neon blue. What we didn't know until we got back to the docks, was the world record for houndfish was only eight pounds, four ounces. Houndfish catches were so rare, that there was only one all class record listed instead of the many line class records listed for most other fish. Sheldon probably had a world record and we didn't even know it. It sure did taste good.

We pulled into the docks just as dark clouds opened up with a tropical shower. We dashed to the tiki bar where ever-friendly staff served fresh houndfish fingers and pina coladas. We sat back and enjoyed the view of the bay, watching boats come in through the mist. My back sure was worn out from fighting all those roosterfish; so I wandered up to the lodge's masseuse and received a great massage to loosen up tight muscles.

At dinner we had multinational discussions of catches, losses, line class records, lures, and fish stories. The world record book of the International Game Fish Association, created by Ernest Hemingway, was passed around to help us target species and line weights to use the next day.

One particular twenty-year-old girl from Japan was honeymooning at the lodge with her parents. The family was intent on breaking world records and had brought their own handmade lures and exotic rods and reels filled with six and eight pound line. The daughter already had several records for exotic species in Japan, and was determined to set more here.

Other groups concentrated on fly-fishing records for sailfish. While no records were set that week, there were many shattered fly rods and stripped reels to show for the effort. I had a hard enough time catching fish on a heavy rod. I did not need to handicap myself with a flimsy fly rod.

The next morning I rolled out of bed at five-thirty, but could barely straighten up my aching back.

After painfully stumbling around the room for a few minutes, I told Greg, "You're going to have to catch that world record without me. I'm hurting too much."

"Okay old man. We'll bring back a story for you."

"I'm going to chill out today by the pool."

Greg and Sheldon went out again for another stellar day of fishing, catching more roosterfish, cubera snapper, and jackfish. I rested by the pool for the morning, then explored the lodge. I talked to Terri Andrews about their airport runway expansion under construction. She was extending the runway from 750 feet to 1,550 feet in order to accommodate corporate jets. She asked if I, being a civil engineer, would look at the construction being performed to check the contractor's quality of work. When I said I would be thrilled to help, Teri quickly organized an expedition.

We took a panga up river to the runway site, where a contractor was transplanting a fifty-foot wide river a few thousand feet to enable the runway extension and to relieve flooding of an adjacent village. The contractor proudly showed me his modern concepts of ditch stabilization, culverts, gabions, and lakes to reconstruct the river in a conservative manner that would be easy to maintain. I was very impressed at the work being performed without the use of construction plans.

We mounted tractors and moved two more miles through the jungle. When we crossed a stream, the tractor fell into a deep hole and whoops, we were stuck. Terri radioed the hotel to send ATVs and backhoes to pull us out. While we waited for the rescue team, I spent a couple of hours exploring the lush jungle. The down time enabled me watch Wounaan Indians pole up the river in dugouts to cut bananas, fish with hand lines, and pan for gold. What a marvelous escape back in time.

That night we had another dinner party and awards celebration. We were served gourmet fish from the grill, stuffed plantains, vegetables (don't ask me what they were) in a red chili sauce, and the piece de resistance - flaming baked Alaska! This was truly a trip of a lifetime.

While we dined under a magical rainforest canopy, awards were given out for biggest fish, most fish, first billfish, and so on. What a wonderful way to finish off the ultimate fishing trip.

That week our fleet caught 468 sailfish and untold numbers of roosterfish. Our boat caught sixty-six fish for the three-day trip, including eight sails, eight roosterfish, twenty-seven bonita, five albacore tuna, one cubera snapper, one grouper, and other assorted species. The staff apologized to us for experiencing an average week of fishing in Pinas Bay. They encouraged us to come back when the fish were biting better.

The abundance of marine life in Pinas Bay was staggering. Tropic Star Lodge's circle-hooks and catch and release policies were shining examples of resource management for the rest of the world to follow. These practices will ensure that great numbers of fish will remain in Pinas Bay. From beginning to end, the splendid service and friendliness of Panamanians made for an unforgettable trip.

Gordon and Doctor Neil at Tropic Star Lodge

Pacific Sail Fish

Roosterfish

Made in the USA
Lexington, KY
14 February 2015